Surviving the Great Medical Care Swindle

Author

Barry Hardy

Surviving the Great Medical Care Swindle

Copyright © 2009 Barry Hardy publications which is part of BH Management Services Ltd, London UK

First Edition published 30th July 2009.

All rights reserved. No part of this book may be reproduced or transmitted in any form or by any means without written permission of the author.

ISBN 978-0-9561538-6-9

Discover more at www.barryhardy.com

I am a mortal living amongst mortals and I too have rights and needs

DECENCY WARNING

Please note that; Surviving the Great Medical Care Swindle contains strong, explicit views including the use of offensive language, which some may find unnecessarily gratuitous. Therefore please don't read this book if you are easily offended by:

- Strong views.
- Strong language.
- Grammatical inconsistencies.

Or

- Personal experiences and perceptions expressed freely.

I have the power in me to be all that I was born to be and now I believe it !

DEDICATION

This book is dedicated to the battalions of helpless souls butchered in the killing fields of medical man. We who survive will do our level best to right their wrongs.

I am a mortal living amongst mortals and I too have rights and needs

DISCLAIMER

The information provided in this book should not be construed as personal medical or clinical advice or instruction no action should be taken based solely on the contents of this book. Readers should consult appropriate professionals on any matter relating to their health and well being. The information and opinions provided here are for personal research purposes only. Readers who fail to consult appropriate professionals assume the risk of incurring injury and must accept any consequences directly or indirectly associated with their personal actions on any and all related matters.

I have the power in me to be all that I was born to be and now I believe it !

Foreword

Apart from birth, taxes and death there is one other more insidious aspect of mortality that very few of us escape from with impunity and that is our interactions with the medical, clinical and surgical world. You see; we're programmed from a very early age to believe that representation from the same have our best interests at heart and are indeed of exemplary stature and character. However it's not until either we or a loved one is struck down by some form of protracted illness that the conscious minority in our society realise that in order to regain our health we must; 'fight back' at the sheer level of deviancy, dogma and incompetence that poisons every aspect of those industries.

This book explores that position and is based upon my own personal points of views that are a derivative and consequence of my own personal battles with the medical, clinical and surgical industries. Points of views; which I respectfully acknowledge are not underwritten by; medical, clinical or surgical qualification but have nevertheless been perfected and underwritten via my own experiences at the hands of fundamentally flawed and even fraudulent representation from the same.

I am a mortal living amongst mortals and I too have rights and needs

I've often been asked recently why I appear to be less than generous towards the medical industry in my books and my answer is that I'm a very generous man where there is good cause. If I come across that I have an axe to grind against the medical industry well perhaps I really do have good cause. You see; I don't have an axe to grind with the medical industry simply because I was failed by one cursory cretin, no! I have an axe to grind because I was failed, abused, misdiagnosed and mistreated for over 30+ years.

Because of that and the fact that actually I've always been a very decent and generous man I passionately believe that there is a need to challenge both the ethical and moral service delivery standards of this industry and to seek redress where they fail us. You see; far too many decent, yet very ill people are being failed and abused daily by this industry whilst luddites within that industry line their pockets at the taxpaying publics' expense. There is no other industry in the developed world that delivers such shoddy, low quality or dogmatically flawed service delivery and customer care as our medical industry does and that's why both it and all the incongruent institutions that underwrite its very existence must be raised to the ground.

It's high time that we had 21st century intellect, attitudes and world class service delivery from our medical industry therein smashing and replacing its 18th century old boy's club culture for good. Because at the moment we're actually funding an industrial culture that's paying people to abuse us and write us off with impunity and to be honest; even basic decency suggests there's something morally wrong with that.

I have the power in me to be all that I was born to be and now I believe it !

Acknowledgments

My sincere thanks go out to:

My lovely Karina without who's love and support for and of me there would have been no mortal redemption or hope for me.

Dr Sarah Myhill and Hania Baker for all their support and generosity towards my wellbeing and clinical care.

Mrs Edna Garrick for her generosity in agreeing to proof read my manuscript for me.

Mr Abdi Nur Ali, Mr. Dahir Nur Ali and Mr Abdikarin Mohamed for their generosity during the compilation of this book in their internet café on Westow Hill.

Finally to all the medical and clinical incompetents that I've encountered thus far, you are the only reason for this books production. I always knew that there was an answer to my problem and having proved that I'm now happy to share it with the world.

I am a mortal living amongst mortals and I too have rights and needs

ESSENTIAL READING

Everything covered in this book draws upon my own detailed personal passage through chronic illness that I cover in my book *Raphael's Legacy*. To ensure that you understand and/or do not either misinterpret or misrepresent any statement, phrase or passage in this book, please ensure that you have read Raphael's Legacy prior to exploring the subtle nuances of this book. It is also important to note that I have covered specific illnesses in a series of books which are derivatives of Raphael's Legacy.

Word of caution, if you haven't read Raphael's Legacy then you must explore at the very least the most relevant single illness book in relation to your chronic illness prior to exploring this book. In that way you can ensure that you fully understand why I say the things I say and why I propose the things in the way that I propose them in this book. For your reference a listing of all those support books is at your disposal on the next page.

Finally and above all things, please ensure that as you move towards better health that you are adequately supported by suitably qualified professional service providers.

I have the power in me to be all that I was born to be and now I believe it !

Further personal insight and self help books written by Barry Hardy include:

Raphael's Legacy
Stress at Close Quarters
Anxiety at Close Quarters
Exploring Fluid Normality
Arthritis at Close Quarters
Raphael Treatment Protocol
Depression at Close Quarters
Fibromyalgia at Close Quarters
Lymes Disease at Close Quarters
Gulf War Syndrome at Close Quarters
Toxic Body Syndrome at Close Quarters
Myalgic Encephalopathy at Close Quarters
Chronic Fatigue Syndrome at Close Quarters
Bipolar / Manic Depression at Close Quarters
Obsessive Compulsive Disorder at Close Quarters

You can purchase any of these books at www.barryhardy.com

I am a mortal living amongst mortals and I too have rights and needs

CONTENTS

Decency warning 3
Dedication 4
Disclaimer 5
Foreword 6
Acknowledgments 8
Essential reading 9
Contents 11
Content brief overview 13
(1) Food for thought! 17
(2) Searching for the truth 21
(3) The darker side of illness 27
(4) Pathetic medical mindsets 35
(5) Hippocratic froth 49
(6) Finding the answers 59
(7) A very personal battle 79

I have the power in me to be all that I was born to be and now I believe it !

(8) Treatments options 95
(9) Analytical testing.. 135
(10) A case for self exploration 139
(11) Mind anger acceptance... 171
(12) Self worth - no pacts.. 177
Decency Warning.. 184

I am a mortal living amongst mortals and I too have rights and needs

CONTENT BRIEF OVERVIEW

This book consists of twelve key sections, where I sequentially begin;

1. Postulating preliminary food for thought on a wide range of health related perceptions, in essence this is; easy reading designed to engender a subtle shift in individual perceptions and in doing so hopefully generate an upbeat state of receptivity.

2. Exploring what it is to search for and understand the truth behind chronic illness, the illusions that are sold, the cruel realities that are all to frequent and the requirements of those committed to securing resolution and a more enhanced state of personal well being.

3. Exploring the darker side of illness which is has nothing to do with any given illness itself. No, the darker side of illness is always the part played by medical, clinical and/or surgical representation. Where you as the patient frequently find yourself being, misdiagnosed, mistreated, abused, written off and blamed for your problem simply because our medical, clinical and/or surgical models allow their representation to do so.

I have the power in me to be all that I was born to be and now I believe it !

4. Exploring the myth that our psychology is the generator and/or originator of all chronic illness states and in doing so proactively advocating the reason for change in our collective perceptions and attitudes towards the medical, clinical and surgical industries from both sufferers and practitioners alike.

5. Exploring the hypocrisy and false truths that we've all been sold by those within the medical, clinical and surgical industries who choose to hide behind the Hippocratic Oath.

6. Exploring the insanity that can be diagnostic analysis, in doing so proactively advocating the reason for change in our collective perceptions and attitudes towards diagnostic testing from both sufferers and practitioners alike.

7. Exploring the obscenity of my own personal interactions with medical, clinical and surgical representation during the course of my desperate unaided battle for a better quality of life, therein prescriptively outlining the reason for change in our collective perceptions and attitudes towards diagnostic testing from both sufferers and practitioners alike.

8. Exploring the myriad of treatment protocols that I had undertook in pursuit of wellness, in doing so proactively advocating the reason for change in our collective perceptions and attitudes towards treatment options from both sufferers and practitioners alike.

I am a mortal living amongst mortals and I too have rights and needs

9. Exploring testing option services that proved beneficial to me and in doing so proactively advocating the reason for change in our collective perceptions and attitudes towards treatment options from both sufferers and practitioners alike.

10. Exploring the process of self exploration looking specifically at, root cause analysis, toxic body syndrome, healing and reaction time lines in doing so proactively advocating the reason for change in our collective perceptions and attitudes towards treatment options from both sufferers and practitioners alike.

11. Exploring the insanity and yet the healthy reality of mind anger towards those with the medical industry who have failed, abused or misdiagnosed in doing so proactively advocating the reason for change in our collective perceptions and attitudes towards treatment options from both sufferers and practitioners alike.

12. Exploring the reality of mortality including the value of self worth in the process of returning to wellness in the sure and self confident knowledge that we don't need to enter into any false reality pacts simply because others seek to, or would wish to rewrite our past, current or futures. As we move towards wellness and/or acceptance, we do not need to exonerate the fragilities of other parties' commitment and/or generosity towards us, our life and our endeavours, because that is something that only they can do for themselves.

I have the power in me to be all that I was born to be and now I believe it !

I am a mortal living amongst mortals and I too have rights and needs

(1) FOOD FOR THOUGHT!

Medical, Clinical & Surgical Worlds

The medical, clinical & surgical world is full of humans each with their own unique gifts, skills and personal flaws and it's because the medical world is full of mortals and not earth God's that they fail us so badly day after day. But don't just sit back any longer when you're abused, let down or failed by anyone from these worlds, sue them, bring them and their industry to account for in doing so you will not only help yourself via the pursuit of redress, but indirectly you'll play a very big part in helping the entire human race. Read more in Raphael's Legacy by Barry Hardy

The Great Psychological Bluff and Scandal

If we allow others to cloud our realities in terms of who we are and what we're actually experiencing with inappropriate postulations about the state of our psychology, be under no illusion we fail ourselves completely at every conceivable level. On matters of psychology when pursuing well-being, listen to your antagonists but choose not to hear when you're being written as another psychological basket case. Because

I have the power in me to be all that I was born to be and now I believe it!

I'm confident you'll discover if you test your body thoroughly, that it's your body that's at fault not your emotions or mind. At that point all psychological assertions can be met head on as you pursue a meaningful life. Read more in Raphael's Treatment Protocol by Barry Hardy

Eminently Solvable Conditions

When you're health conditions are being fudged and written off as illnesses that have only names with no treatment or resolution options open or offered to you to help you get by or simply cope. You really have only two options open to you and that is to stick with what you've got if that's all you can do or you can test and test until your condition or conditions are identified. We are all the sole guardians of our own mortality; therefore we can either relinquish our responsibility to the uncaring and obscene or we can fight for what is our mortal right, the right to decency and an acceptable quality of life. Read more in Exploring Fluid Normality by Barry Hardy

Depression Expression

There is no insanity at all in depression expression save only for the sheer depth of suffering its victims incur. Because the reality is that depression expression can be eradicated in days, not weeks, months or years when the physical generators, precursors and accelerators of depression expression are treated and removed. All that is needed is a shift in perceptions, a position significantly enhanced by holistic treatment results. Read more in Depression at Close Quarters by Barry Hardy

I am a mortal living amongst mortals and I too have rights and needs

Stressful Resolution

Whilst the majority of us have experienced some degree of stress at some point in our life, very few of us realise that it's so predictable, so treatable and so recoverable from, hence nothing whatsoever for us all to get stressed about. Once you understand the dynamics, your stress levels will fall and at that point you will wonder why you allowed yourself to get so stressed in the first place or indeed at all. Read more in Stress at Close Quarters by Barry Hardy

Wellness

There is no great secret to wellness over and above understanding the root cause of any decline from wellness into un-wellness. But that root-cause analysis is not determined by non intrusive subjective analysis, because it can only be determined by holistic, scientific testing and analysis. Anything less than that is mere supposition, supposition however has never cured anyone or created a state of considered wellbeing, but it has forced many poor mortals like you, me and us, to give up completely on the idea of a satisfying mortality. Read more in Raphael's Legacy by Barry Hardy

I have the power in me to be all that I was born to be and now I believe it !

Divine or Higher Force

We all at some point need someone or something to pray to, no matter what race or creed we originate from. But the reality is when all said and done, we all as mortals are the only living beings able to solve complex mortal mysteries, so whilst it's okay I suspect to offer up prayers. I think it best that we all put our faith in ourselves and the endeavours of our fellow men. Read more in Raphael's Legacy by Barry Hardy

I am a mortal living amongst mortals and I too have rights and needs

(2) SEARCHING FOR THE TRUTH

No living man knows what mortality in all its normality truly is, until he has been either forced to endure and/or blessed to survive the absurdity and sheer intolerability of apparently irresolvable chronic ill health. For that is a place where no fellow man hears any heartfelt and/or desperate pleas for help, because in that place and in that space there is not one ounce or shred of humanistic decency. It is a place where your body apparently delights in tormenting your very existence and a place where medics with sickening guile, spew their ignorant dogma to you and about you but offer absolutely no help, support or hope for the entirety of your passage through that place.

Such is the depravity of that place and space that; release from mortality becomes an overriding preoccupation for anyone unfortunate enough to find themselves trapped within the same. It is a place where the light refuses to shine with endless penchant, for it is eclipsed almost continually by the purgatory of mortality in and of simply monumental proportions. So let's be very clear here, let no man in your presence ever attempt to liken this place and space with the simplicity of any given minor mortal imposition. For true mortal suffering under whatever presentation it chooses to manifest itself, is not a club or requiring of any arm bands of unity or honour.

I have the power in me to be all that I was born to be and now I believe it !

Because it is a place and time in your mortal passage that is as depraved and dark as mortal suffering can be.

All that being said; I believe that mortal suffering is an unacceptable blight upon the reality of mortality which we must do our level best to eradicate from society if we do nothing else over the next 100 years. Because whilst it may well be a natural dynamic of normal mortality. Simply accepting mortal suffering in any way shape or form because it makes the lives of others much easier is both ethically and morally reprehensible. My personal experiences at the hands of the medical industry continue to generate grave reservations in me about the integrity, decency, credibility and morality of those engaged in medicine and that's why I implore kindred souls to take great care when interacting with the same. You see; only those who have suffered at the hands of the medical industry and yet somehow also managed to survive their so called care' are able to personally validate just how despicably poor, unsupportive and divisive that industry truly is. It is an industry rotten to the core and lacking collaterally in any tangible intellect, integrity and decency across the board and that's why I was forced to explore my own mortality and therein document my chronic ill health resolution in my books. Because whilst I cannot right any wrongs committed to me by my fellow man. The truth of the matter is that as a mortal living amongst mortals' social intercourse with our medical industry is almost certainly heading our way in any one of a hundred forms in the not too distant future and that I'm afraid to say is fact.

I am a mortal living amongst mortals and I too have rights and needs

Nevertheless the questions I believe that you the reader will be better able to ask yourself once you've read this book are; do I believe what any medic is saying to me now and/or in the future and more importantly; have I ever been told the truth at any point in my life by a medic? You see; truths present themselves in many differing forms i.e. the intellectualized truth, the dogmatic truth, the cultural truth and/or the politically motivated truth. However it's not until we've either tested the validity and/or experienced the stupidity of any given truth that we're in the best possible position to judge and hence re-evaluate the truth of any given truth that we've previously allowed ourselves to believe. Because of that you may even read this book and think blimey this guy is a complete waste of space and off his head or indeed you may even think; 'hmnnnn some of this makes sense, and because of that I'm willing to explore my own perceptions.

Either way;

It doesn't really make any difference to me what you think about me, about my ideas and/or my postulations for wellbeing in the greater scheme of things. Because all that should be important to you as a chronic illness sufferer is how best you can improve your current quality of life if it is in anyway lacking vitality. All I will ever say in my own personal defense is that unlike some of the procrastinating numpties (*self obsessed theorizing so called experts and/or self appointed experts*) that we all have the potential to meet along the way from the medical industry. I've actually walked my talk and healed myself, whilst other so called enlightened experts simply sat back, abused me and wrote me off.

I have the power in me to be all that I was born to be and now I believe it !

So that now and after one hellish struggle for better health, it is my considered belief that chronic illness is nothing more than an expression of disease and therefore does not originate from insanity or emotional instability. Accept that and you're at least part of the way to understanding that; the originators of chronic illness are always;

    a. Physical diseases and/or rarely injury to the brain.

Or

    b. Bodily process failure and/or deviations from normal functioning.

Or

    c. Inflammation generated through diseases or injury.

Or

    d. Toxic body syndrome generated through, physical disease, bodily process failure and/or deviations from normal functioning and Inflammation generated through diseases or injury.

So then; if you're currently suffering from any form of chronic illness and/or have suffered from a chronic illness condition in the past and wish to unravel the truth about everything associated with that expression of disease, then perhaps you should;

- Stay open and consider fully any and all of my postulations for the pursuit of well-being that I explore, before deciding upon the most appropriate approach or course of action for you.

And

- Always work with or at least consult with; a suitably qualified service provider before making changes to any or all of your current treatment protocols.

But

- Under NO circumstance must you STOP taking or STOP participating in any treatment protocol designed to support your wellbeing in the absence of suitable qualified service provider because to do so would be foolish and irresponsible and you could put your long term wellbeing at significant risk.

I have the power in me to be all that I was born to be and now I believe it !

The ultimate goal for anyone suffering from a chronic illness must be the return to optimum health; however no one can ever hope to regain a level of optimum health if they fail to or are not prepared to search for and qualify the root cause of their illness.

I am a mortal living amongst mortals and I too have rights and needs

(3) THE DARKER SIDE OF ILLNESS

You may be surprised to read this, but let me send a shock wave racing right through your body because I'm going to empower you with a very distasteful truth. You see, at the point you move into a state of chronic ill health the deadliest people you will ever meet are those who work within and/or who support the medical/clinical world. So much so that I'm somewhat embarrassed these days by the fact that whilst many turned their back during the greedy and wasted Thatcher and Major years. I spent a great deal of my youth campaigning and lobbying against local and central government with passion on a whole host of issues, not least to save what I felt was a laudable institution under threat, namely our glorious NHS. 'Boy did I get it wrong'. The institution and all the mechanisms that underpin that bullshit ridden and sedentary industry are rotten to the core.

Fortunately I have no medical or clinical qualifications, I'm just a regular guy trained in engineering and engineering sciences and like most engineers I have an engaging and problem solving mind. As a regular guy, albeit with a little bit of professional training, I would respectfully suggest that having an enquiring, capable and problem solving mind is probably the most rudimentary of all mandatory requirements for all those engaged in a key service delivery profession such as the medical industry.

I have the power in me to be all that I was born to be and now I believe it !

Now clearly the back room girls and boys of that industry appear to have that predisposition because we have all witnessed the tremendous advances that have been achieved over the past fifty years or so. I'm talking here however about medical scientists and scientific medical engineers, the people we should regard as the true heroes of medicine, the men and woman who steadfastly develop new tools, new tests, new treatments, new techniques and new machines etc, for the betterment of man. However, the heroes of medicine are a stark contrast to the front end 'luddites' i.e. *Any Opponent of Industrial Change or Innovation* of the medical world that we the general public are unfortunately exposed to. The people that we're exposed to are only interested in one thing and one thing only: self gratification at the expense of their fellow man. I refer of course to the medical receptionist, the nurse, the general practitioner, the registrar, the specialist and the consultant. They may or may not start off life as self protectionist 'luddites' but at the point they're allowed to administer their own unique brand of divisive, destructive and judgmental clinical administration and medical butchery up the innocent public, they move into that 'luddite' mindset wholesale.

These people are guilty of crimes against humanity that simply eclipse the acts and transgressions of the worst of all ruthless dictators. They are institutionally lazy, self obsessed, greedy, serial abusers with only one thing on their agenda, self preservation of their highly inflated status within what is the devil's own institutions. Forget any waffle about the Hippocratic oath than anyone from this industry chooses to offload onto you, the bottom line for these people is themselves first, themselves second and whatever is left over; is all for themselves. These people don't solve problems, they don't hear suffering, they're not prepared to think outside of the box and why?

I am a mortal living amongst mortals and I too have rights and needs

Well because they're the wrong people for the job, the wrong people who are gaining great rewards from an industry that is rotten to the core. For anyone misfortunate enough to develop a chronic illness I've mapped the actual clinical abuse process that most people are forced to endure during the course of their chronic illness at the end of this chapter. What the process loop cannot do is qualify the simply appalling nature, neglect and abandonment anyone experiences during that process. Where the cause of desperate conditions are often written off as psychological issues and placed directly back on the shoulders of the patients, identifying them as the originator and hence owner of the condition in totality. That being said; it's eminently justifiable to suggest that the selection criteria for individuals entering the medical industry and the training they undergo are now by modern day standards both outdated and fundamentally flawed. Because if the selection criteria for those entering the medical industry and their subsequent training were right; then we wouldn't have such a fundamentally flawed service and individuals who go onto develop chronic illness wouldn't simply be written off.

I have the power in me to be all that I was born to be and now I believe it !

You only need to be misfortunate enough to become ill to discover just how diabolically poor, unresponsive and uncooperative this industry really is. No matter which sector you seek help from, be it either the public or the private sectors, the service is abominable. No matter whom you consult or what level that representative may be, it doesn't matter what tests you participate in or what sort of investigation you undergo. These people know very little about very little and what they do know or articulate freely to you is generally outdated, self protectionist and complete and utter rubbish with no humanistic element to it. You see:

- How can it be that we still have a sociologically biased industry that is controlled from within?

- How can it be that we still have a sociologically biased industry that protects and rewards underperformance from those who support it or are employed by it?

- How can it be that we still have a sociologically biased industry that is afraid to acknowledge advancement in thinking until that change in approach is decades old?

- How can it be that we still have a sociologically biased industry where those who are employed in it have no idea about the majority of diseases and conditions they encounter?

- How can it be that every unexplainable condition can be written off by those within this industry as simply being of a psychological origin?

I am a mortal living amongst mortals and I too have rights and needs

- How can it be that they're programmed as a service provider within this industry not to hear, help or support suffering and pain?

- How can it be that no matter what your own personal or professional credentials are, as soon as you engage with this industry you're immediately considered an intellectual cretin by those providing basic services within?

- How can it be that if you dare to challenge this industry from within you're immediately risking your career?

- How can it be that fighting for resolution from chronic illness can expose you to the pressure of clinical services being withdrawn from you?

I have the power in me to be all that I was born to be and now I believe it !

And yet they all assume the same grotesque air of arrogance about who they are and what they are and how complicated your particular situation may or may not be. This bullshit they offload is by default, simply an outdated facade designed for a bygone age when we the general public were considered as intellectually inferior to representation from this industry. But this misguided assumption still exists today to mask clear inadequacies, ignorance and fragile egos yet the reality is that it's probably more disrespectful to us now than it ever was because we're all much smarter than this industry gives us credit for. This crux of my irritation is that this industry and those who support it are an affront to everything that is both decent and good in our modern world. We don't expect or accept bullshit and ridicule from any other private sector or public service industry. So why do we accept this institutional misconduct from the clinical world?

Well, the truth is that we really don't think that we have any power to change our situation and at the point we commence any social intercourse with this industry we're already in a state of vulnerability and low vitality. Therein resides the reason why so many people with undiagnosed disease states go onto to develop chronic illness before ultimately being written off as a neurotic or a depressive with no possible chance of making an effective recovery. You see the medical/clinical industry is very adept at falsely blaming the symptoms of chronic disease states and ultimately Depression etc, upon the fragile psychology of any mortal who presents with life debilitating symptoms and conditions. But what is the truth behind this predisposition of our psychology being the root cause of all our chronic illness and chronic illness expression? Well I'm going to look at that very point in the next chapter so please fasten your seat belt, but first check out surviving the ignorant clinical abuse loop on the next page.

I am a mortal living amongst mortals and I too have rights and needs

Surviving The Great Medical Care Swindle

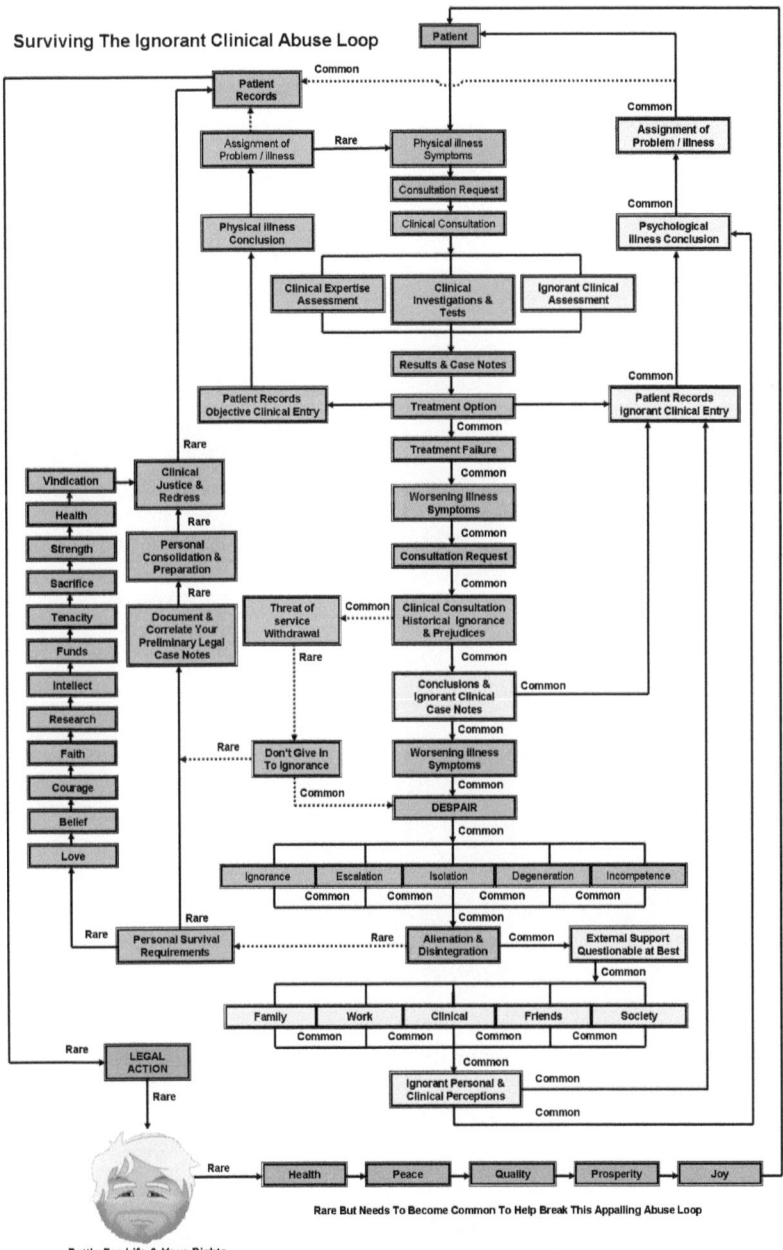

I have the power in me to be all that I was born to be and now I believe it!

Personal Notes Page

I am a mortal living amongst mortals and I too have rights and needs

(4) Pathetic medical mindsets

How frequent is it for patients' problems and in particular chronic illness expression to be simply written off as nothing more than a deluded psychology? Well far more frequently than you may expect. You see, there is a prescriptive culture within the medical world which has a predisposition for looking to offload all the patients' problems back onto them. It's basically part of the overall clinical abuse model and its guiding principles are no more than:

- When in doubt just call your patients illness a psychological problem.

- When tests don't indicate a deviation from normal values, just call your patients' illnesses a psychological problem.

- When imaging doesn't show up any abnormalities just call your patients' illnesses a psychological problem.

- When you simply can't be bothered with your patients' preposterous symptoms just call they're illness a psychological problem.

I have the power in me to be all that I was born to be and now I believe it !

But what is the truth and just what part does our psychology play in the bigger scheme of things when it comes to our health? Well first we need to understand that whilst we may be familiar with the term 'psychological illness', few of us know that the modern day originator of this scientific field was 'Wilhelm Wundt' who established the first psychology lab in Leipzig, Germany. Believing at the time that *properly* trained individuals should be able to *accurately* identify the mental processes that accompanied an individual's feelings, sensations, and thoughts.

The emphasis here is upon properly trained individuals accurately identifying the processes that underpin the emotional predisposition of individuals in any given psychological state. Now the development of this science didn't happen by chance, mankind in all its societies has battled for centuries with the thorny issue of mental illness and insanity. That's why we in the United Kingdom still have such draconian measures as the 'Mental Health Act' where citizens can be sectioned and detained under said act for extended periods if they pose either a danger to others or more often than not simply a danger to themselves.

Now there is absolutely no doubt that some individuals are insane, we see that in the likes of Shipman, Stalin, Hitler and Saddam Hussein etc. But the problem is there have been no major advances since time began to delineate between organic insanity and biologically insults that have the propensity to inflict insanity or in other words chronic illness expression upon mankind. So we still have no way of knowing who's insane and who's simply biologically ill. I'm advocating therefore that the golden psychological card which is so readily used to explain the unexplainable illness i.e. there is a significant psychological component to your illness, is simply a complete red herring in the majority of chronic illnesses and certainly in the majority of depressions expression situations.

I am a mortal living amongst mortals and I too have rights and needs

Those inaccurate value judgments simply have no clinical grounding upon which to base the assumptions of a psychological condition upon save for some cursory presenting symptoms. Now it's that point of clinical evidence that I wish firstly to focus upon. You see; if you present yourself to a medic suspecting that you have let's say; hypothyroidism or Lymes Disease etc. The first thing they will do is:

(a) Poo poo and ridicule you.

And then

(b) Perhaps agree reluctantly to give you some very basic blood tests.

They will then rattle on about how they couldn't possibly give you a trial of low dose thyroid medication or antibiotics until your tests results come back and prove that you do indeed have an issue with either your thyroid or Lymes Disease. Yet the same medical practitioner within 5 minutes of another consultation will conclude with NO clinical data that you are indeed suffering from a psychological condition and therein he or she will feel eminently comfortable to prescribe anyone of a line of toxic psychiatric substances. It seems to me incredulous in the 21st century, that some unqualified medic can make such sweeping statements about the condition of someone's psychology. More so when we realise that the vast majority of medics have very little if any psychological or psychiatric training.

I have the power in me to be all that I was born to be and now I believe it !

It's clearly apparent to me now after years of suffering at the hands of this industry that in bog standard, tricky or complex medical investigation situations we the patients are always to a greater extent perceived to be the responsible party for the clinical problem we're experiencing because as mere mortals we have such fragile psychologies. Surely though this situation is truly insane, how can this industry say on one hand that, unless their outdated investigation techniques are able to detect a problem then it simply doesn't exist whilst in the same breath assign clinical labels to patients with the shallowest to zero investigations of their case? I do not argue or disagree with the fact that our psychology plays a very big part in the way we cope with, or handle our difficulties. But it is not the root cause of all mans hidden or seemingly translucent diseases and I therefore repudiate the waving of the psychological cause golden card by poorly trained representatives from within the medical industry.

If our psychology was the root cause of the majority of illnesses then we would be able to see for ourselves the advances in the treatment of psychological conditions over the past hundred years. Because the money we spend on this aspect of medical care via so called research and residential care etc, is simply insane. The reality to my primary postulation is quite stark and I say that because the medical industry is having a laugh. Nothing much has changed in the diagnosis and treatment of these conditions despite the oceans of scientific papers that have been written. There have been no major breakthroughs in clinical analysis, qualification or treatments of psychological conditions save for commercially sponsored indoctrination and use of debatably successful drugs.

I am a mortal living amongst mortals and I too have rights and needs

Now if anyone who has been put on those drugs has improved, all I can say is good for you, but for the majority of us who didn't need them in our body to solve our health condition, then I would respectfully suggest that they are:

- Dangerous

Or

- Complete waste of bloody time.

The medical world's view remains without any validity that all illness derives from an emotional or mental state and that physical illness if it cannot be pinpointed simply doesn't exist. But surely these are the views of yesterday's men, the sorts who questioned the scientific validity of thoughts about;

- The Earth.
- The Sun.
- The Moon.
- The Stars

I have the power in me to be all that I was born to be and now I believe it !

They are the views of men who dared not seek to discover if the world was flat or round and who shouted heresy if a man sort to make representation or postulate different thoughts or articulated and challenged perceived truths. The very fact that this approach happens almost by default in clinical surgeries throughout the UK, simply validates my position that the medical world is seemingly still stuck in the dark ages, ignorant and despite its protestations, doesn't really care. Were they motor mechanics or plumbers with the same approach to problems these people would be simply unemployable or even in jail i.e.

- 'I'm sorry Mr. Hardy but I couldn't find anything wrong with your car/boiler, but incidentally have you ever tried counselling, sometimes it really does help?'

Or what about this favourite one;

- 'Yes I hear what you say Mr. Hardy but that is just a sensation of knocking at the front of your car, I'm the expert here I can't find any signs of knocking so perhaps its more of a psychological issue than you think, how's your sex life by the way?'

Two months later the engine in my car implodes or my boiler stops working;

- 'Oh well these things just happen sometimes Mr. Hardy, I've checked your notes and it would appear that your tyres and exhaust were fine/your pipework and radiators were fine when you were last in here, now you're clearly agitated so I'm going to suggest that there seems more to this than just an engine in your car/boiler not working, do you think you need to see a psychiatrist?'

- 'Answer, no I don't think I should see a psychiatrist you complete waste of space, I was in here not so long ago and I told you that there was something seriously wrong with my engine/boiler and all you did was check my tyre pressure and exhaust mounting/my radiator mountings now I'm back here today with a damaged engine/boiler and I'm asking you this, are you a bloody motor mechanic/plumber mate or simply a motor mechanic/plumber on your great grandmothers side of your family?'

The thing is if this happened in real life we would be straight to trading standards but when it comes to the medical industry we're all very guilty of not being prepared to take our abusers on. But the truth of the matter is that the average medic you will ever encounter has little to no training in either psychological or matters of psychiatry and as such are the least qualified of clinicians to prescribe conditions of that nature to you or about you. Yet they have bought into ignorant schools of thought which date way back to the 1920's. Outdated schools of thought that postulated that we, as individuals, are responsible for all our own thoughts and our perceptions on life and that we all have demons and un-

I have the power in me to be all that I was born to be and now I believe it !

reconciled issues deep with in us that frequently manifest themselves as illness. Today that belief is still perpetuated by our ignorant medics as a way of offloading the cause of a tricky problem back onto the shoulders of its originator simply because they know that they can do that. So much so that you can bet your last £10 that if you encounter any extended or unexplainable medical issue or period of chronic Depression that it will be the obligatory psychological postulations or dogma that are rolled out or recorded on your medical records. All based upon a fundamentally flawed platform of:

- Personality Psychology – This specialist area looks at the various elements that make up individual personalities and includes Freud's structural model of personality as an example of a protagonist of this field.

However at the point a qualified psychologist is brought onto your case I can guarantee you that Personality Psychology which has already been used by medical ignoramuses as ammunition against you will be almost entirely dropped in favour of:

- Clinical Psychology Investigations – This specialty area is focused on the assessment, diagnosis, and treatment of mental disorders.

However the study of psychology has moved on tremendously since its conception and there are now many widely differing schools of thought and differing approaches to this challenging subject including:

I am a mortal living amongst mortals and I too have rights and needs

- Cognitive Psychology – This specialist area is the study of human thought processes and cognitions, including topics such as attention, memory, perception, decision-making, problem solving, and language acquisition.

- Abnormal Psychology - This specialty area is focused on research and treatment of a variety of mental disorders and is linked to psychotherapy and clinical psychology.

- Social Psychology – This specialist area is a discipline that uses scientific methods to study social influence, social perception, and social interaction. Social psychology studies diverse subjects including group behaviour, social perception, leadership, nonverbal behaviour, conformity, aggression, and prejudice.

- Comparative Psychology – This specialist area is the branch of psychology concerned with the study of animal behaviour, believing that the study of animal behaviour can lead to a deeper and broader understanding of human psychology.

- Forensic Psychology – This specialist area is an applied field focused on using psychological research and principles in the legal and criminal justice system.

I have the power in me to be all that I was born to be and now I believe it !

- Industrial-Organizational Psychology – This specialist area uses psychological research to enhance work performance, select employee, improve product design, and enhance usability.

- Developmental Psychology – This specialist area is the branch of psychology that looks at human growth and development over the lifespan. Theories often focus on the development of cognitive abilities, morality, social functioning, identity, and other life areas.

- School Psychology – This specialist area is the branch of psychology that works within the educational system to help children with emotional, social, and academic issues.

- Biological Psychology - This approach is the only area of accessible psychology that studies how biological processes influence the mind and behaviour.

Ironically though; Biological Psychology will never be rolled out unless you've been through surgery, a crash or a smash. Yet this approach is the only area of accessible psychology that studies how biological processes influence the mind and behaviour. Now there's no getting away from it *Biological Psychology* is still light years away from where it should be by now but at least it's sort of heading in the right direction. The only problem is as ever when undergoing medical interventions, your future will depend entirely upon the training of the psychologist responsible for driving any biological investigations. You may well find that in most instances he or she just simply reverts back to or refers you to another Clinical Psychologist on the grounds of costs or insufficient

I am a mortal living amongst mortals and I too have rights and needs

evidence to warrant extensive testing. Throughout my darkest days I battled like a Spartan albeit a very ill Spartan to find the root cause of my illness and chronic illness expression and yet I was frequently told by medical representatives, 'no we're not testing you for this or for that'. Or 'we can't keep on testing for different things indefinitely Mr. Hardy you're simply going to have to understand that you have a psychiatric problem'.

Now there is absolutely no doubt that if we feel low it's difficult for us to feel happy until we shift our mind set. We see that day after day in the emotions and moods of ourselves and our kith and kin. So how simple would life be if all we needed to do when we were feeling low was to change our mindset just like that. But life as we know is not like that, we are not like that, there are always impositions placed upon our bodies which make it impossible for us to feel happy simply as and when we choose to feel happy. The best we can ever hope to do is to recognize and accept that we have a part to play in that process yet understand that we do not always hold all the keys. So the question remains, is 'psychological illness real or simply a medical form of illness fiction? Well there's no doubt in my mind that there are many forms of psychological illness, but in the absence of firm biological data I cannot accept or agree that psychological illness is an illness in its own right. If the root course of a problem cannot be qualified then it MUST fall into the category of symptoms from an unknown disease. Therein there must be a concerted effort made to search out the origin of that disease and not simply to attempt to treat the symptoms with dangerous views, perceptions or drugs. Under no circumstance can an unknown disease be morally written off as an emotional or psychological illness because I would respectfully suggest that act in itself constitutes gross clinical malpractice.

I have the power in me to be all that I was born to be and now I believe it !

I therefore advocate that anyone being written off by a medical representative, must document that incident via a formal communiqué to their practice in readiness for future legal action. It is only at the point we start bringing the medical industry to account, day after day that we will:

- Get the services we so desperately need.

And

- Weed out the 'luddites' who shouldn't be in the industry in the first place.

The global market place we live and work in is full of medics desperately looking to explore new boundaries. So if we don't have the quality home grown medics that we need who are prepared to accept that we're all part of the 21st century. Then I say, lets simply offload the; 'incompetents' from that industry to the unemployed wastelands where they belong and lets import brighter, fresher service support professionals as we would do with plumbers, builders, electrician and engineers. We simply don't have the time, money or resolve to bring the 'luddite' bastions of our medical industry kicking and screaming into line with our modern needs, standards and expectations. We need effective medical services now, not light years from now, but tomorrow, or at the very latest the early part of next week. Personal redress for the underperformance and failures in due diligence are the only way that we, the taxpaying public are ever going to be able to move the medical industry forward kicking and screaming into the modern world. When a medic fails you when you're in a chronic state of illness, complain about his/her conduct and then sue them if needs must, when a medic fails a loved one of yours in a chronic state of illness, complain about his/her conduct and then sue them if needs must. Let's collectively generate a real state of fear for the 'luddites' who generate great rewards for themselves from this industry for in doing so:

> (a) We will bring about the changes that we need in terms of securing a world class holistic professional service delivery from this industry.

And

> (b) We will generate a culture where protectionist old boys clubs are smashed completely by default and for good.

If we all commit to this process, I'm looking forward too and optimistic that following generations will not need to suffer like we have, at the hands of 'luddites' who secure great riches and status from working with the Devils own Institutions.

I have the power in me to be all that I was born to be and now I believe it !

I am a mortal living amongst mortals and I too have rights and needs

(5) Hippocratic Froth

One of the most laughable things I've found about the scum ridden corridors of the medical industry is that it is always blowing hot and cold. One minute its postulating higher ethical values and the preservation of life and the next minute it's refusing to treat patients on the grounds of:

- Cost

- Flawed diagnosis.

- Personal prejudices.

- Anything that's flavour of the month.

We've all read and heard about cases of people losing loved ones because a medic or series of medics simply couldn't be arsed to do the job they're paid to do. What may not be apparent however at the point a clinical case failure is brought to our attention is the sheer hell that the patients' family has had to work through in an attempt to seek redress for their loved one's injustice.

I have the power in me to be all that I was born to be and now I believe it !

But why is it so hard to seek redress for shoddy care, we put our lives in these people's hands because we think that they know what they're doing. So when it's obvious they've screwed up surely they should just hold their hands up and come clean, in line with the principles of the Hippocratic Oath. That isn't, I would suggest, too much for us to ask of them is it? Well the truth is I'm afraid it is.

You see even when the medical industry or one of its representatives get it wrong they simply can't hold up their hands and say I or we got it wrong. They may even have known for some time that they have a weak member of staff in their midst who is or could be jeopardizing peoples' lives, but it's not part of the industry's psyche to stand up and proactively address 'shit performance'. What invariably happens is that the old boys club kicks in and self preservation remains the order of the day.

How many times have you seen and heard news reports where a so called medical expert is simply spewing verbal diarrhea in defense of the indefensible. With either a semi self-humbling posture or an arrogant parental disposition where he or she will rattle on about how sorry they are, and how everyone had done their best for the patient but that this was just an isolated case. But the plain fact of the matter is that too many patients are dying who shouldn't be dying under the care of these shits and what's more; too many patients are being written off who should be living rewarding and happy lives.

I am a mortal living amongst mortals and I too have rights and needs

Nevertheless; I'm confident however that as we begin to clear the debris from years of cover up after cover up we will find that there is no such thing as an isolated incident of failure of due diligence when we're in clinical care. I'm confident based upon my own personal experiences that we will unfortunately discover that it's an endemic theme of poor service delivery. Or in my granddads words; *'At the point you get ill son or are silly enough to get old, you're no longer a person son you're nothing more than a piece of meat on the chopping board of life son and no one really cares'.*

But what is the problem here? And why does this situation exist? Well the answer is simple; the Hippocratic Oath is a myth. Well that last line is not fair really because the Hippocratic Oath is not a myth and you can read a translated version of it later in this chapter if you wish. The real myth is that vast majority of those engaged in medical or clinical work have never signed onto and have never been compelled to sign up to a Hippocratic Oath to allow them to practice. Therein resides the myth, you see, the rogues that we encounter who talk about upholding its values are the very same rogues who by matter of course break all its principles daily. In essence we're being spun a line of thought which is a crude fabrication and not an ethical reality. This is because in truth, as far as we the patients are concerned the Hippocratic Oath simply doesn't exist. Medics simply do what's best for themselves and to hell with the patients in their care. So should we make our medical staff sign up to a modern Hippocratic Oath? Well in truth I don't' really care if they do or they don't, for an Oath is no more than a joke to me when its signed up to by self obsessed cretins and oafs.

I have the power in me to be all that I was born to be and now I believe it !

What I won't to see is:

- Deregulation of the industry.

- I want to see greater clinical accountability.

- I want better training and greater clarity in the selection processes for anyone thinking of joining that industry.

- I want ease of access to all things medical without the clap trap, bullshit and the golden psychology card.

Only when we've moved this industry kicking and screaming into the 21st century can we rid ourselves once and for all of the pompous, arrogant and incompetent service delivery that has been up to now society's greatest medical disease e.g. the people who work within the industry. Just in case you're ever in a sticky situation with a medical representative where the individual is prescriptively using the Hippocratic Oath to validate something they're saying. I've enclosed both an old and a new example of the same to help you determine for yourself if that person actuality lives in entirety the principles enshrined within. On the next page is the oldest version or translation of the Hippocratic Oath that I could find on the web.

I am a mortal living amongst mortals and I too have rights and needs

Older Version of the Oath

I swear by Apollo Physician and Asclepius and Hygieia and Panaceia and all the gods and goddesses, making them my witnesses, that I will fulfill according to my ability and judgment this oath and this covenant: To hold him who has taught me this art as equal to my parents and to live my life in partnership with him, and if he is in need of money to give him a share of mine, and to regard his offspring as equal to my brothers in male lineage and to teach them this art - if they desire to learn it - without fee and covenant; to give a share of precepts and oral instruction and all the other learning to my sons and to the sons of him who has instructed me and to pupils who have signed the covenant and have taken an oath according to the medical law, but no one else. I will apply dietetic measures for the benefit of the sick according to my ability and judgment; I will keep them from harm and injustice. I will neither give a deadly drug to anybody who asked for it, nor will I make a suggestion to this effect. Similarly I will not give to a woman an abortive remedy. In purity and holiness I will guard my life and my art. I will not use the knife, not even on sufferers from stone, but will withdraw in favour of such men as are engaged in this work. Whatever houses I may visit, I will come for the benefit of the sick, remaining free of all intentional injustice, of all mischief and in particular of sexual relations with both female and male persons, be they free or slaves. What I may see or hear in the course of the treatment or even outside of the treatment in regard to the life of men, which on no account one must spread abroad, I will keep to myself, holding such things shameful to be spoken about. If I fulfill this oath and do not violate it, may it be granted to me to enjoy life and art, being honoured with fame among all men for all time to come; if I transgress it and swear falsely, may the opposite of all this be my lot.

I have the power in me to be all that I was born to be and now I believe it !

Now here is a draft transcript of the only modern version I could find of the Hippocratic Declaration created for those passing through Imperial College School of Medicine. I'm unclear if this was ever adopted but it was complied I assume to focus the minds of the recently trained in terms of providing an honourable service……..yeah that right, where at?

Refined Version of the Oath

I solemnly promise that I will to the best of my ability serve humanity caring for the sick, promoting good health, and alleviating pain and suffering. I recognise that the practice of medicine is a privilege with which comes considerable responsibility and I will not abuse my position. I will practise medicine with integrity, humility, honesty, and compassion working with my fellow doctors and other colleagues to meet the needs of my patients. I shall never intentionally do or administer anything to the overall harm of my patients. I will not permit considerations of gender, race, religion, political affiliation, sexual orientation, nationality, or social standing to influence my duty of care. I will oppose policies in breach of human rights and will not participate in them. I will strive to change laws that are contrary to my profession's ethics and will work towards a fairer distribution of health resources. I will assist my patients to make informed decisions that coincide with their own values and beliefs and will uphold patient confidentiality. I will recognise the limits of my knowledge and seek to maintain and increase my understanding and skills throughout my professional life. I will acknowledge and try to remedy my own mistakes and honestly assess and respond to those of others. I will seek to promote the advancement of medical knowledge through teaching and research. I make this declaration solemnly, freely, and upon my honor.

I am a mortal living amongst mortals and I too have rights and needs

Sweet eh? Fine fine words! But I wonder just how much of this froth and rubbish they'll actually manage or be willing to uphold once they're on the fat, greedy, pompous medical gravy train which is to be their life. Who knows, perhaps they will uphold it all with a bit of luck or then again perhaps they simply stick to the bits that make life easier for them. Perhaps I'm just too cynical now, but then again, I do have good cause. The fact of the matter is that I have a dreadful illness which could so easily have been prevented and a genetic condition which makes my life exceedingly difficult but I've never experienced the inspiring principle of the Hippocratic Oath applied to my case. You see, I've never ever wanted anything from this industry save for its representatives to be:

- Technically and clinically competent.

- Decent, honourable and true.

- Interested in solving problems instead of offloading my problems back onto me.

I would never have felt the need to be so disrespectful if I had any respect for this industry at all, but I've been on a treadmill for years now where I've tried to engage with, begged and even demanded from this industry and all to no avail. No matter where I go or who I see the answer is always the same, *'Yes I hear what you say Mr. Hardy but I'm afraid you're not listening, the only problem you have because I've read all your reports are the psychological problems in your head'.*

- Where are all the heroes?

- Where are our service delivery ethics that are enshrined in the Hippocratic Oath?

I have the power in me to be all that I was born to be and now I believe it !

- Why are we the hard working masses, paying so much to underwrite a privileged yet dysfunctional load of crap?

Well I have to say that there are few industries in the modern world today where governments tread so lightly, but this is one that our governments MUST get to grips with once and for all. Because this industry actually believes that both it and those who work in it are actually above due diligence and matters of personal well being and state supported clinical care.

But let's change that flawed perception Ladies and Gents and let's change that starting today, let's bring the bastards who fail us kicking and screaming into the reality that we ourselves are forced to live in every single day. Let's start wrecking the lives and careers of medical rogues if there is good cause or grounds of failure of due diligence can be proven. Because the people who wrecked my bloody life are still out there wrecking the lives of many more people right now.

Personal redress for the underperformance and failures in due diligence are the only way that we, the taxpaying public are ever going to be able to move the medical industry forward kicking and screaming into the modern world.

Therefore when a medic fails you, complain about his or her conduct and then sue them if needs must. When a medic fails a loved one of yours, complain about his or her conduct and then sue them if needs must. Let's collectively generate a real state of fear for these rogues for in doing so:

I am a mortal living amongst mortals and I too have rights and needs

(a) We will bring about the changes that we need in terms of securing a world class holistic professional service delivery from this industry.

And

(b) We will generate a culture where protectionist old boys clubs are smashed completely by default and for good.

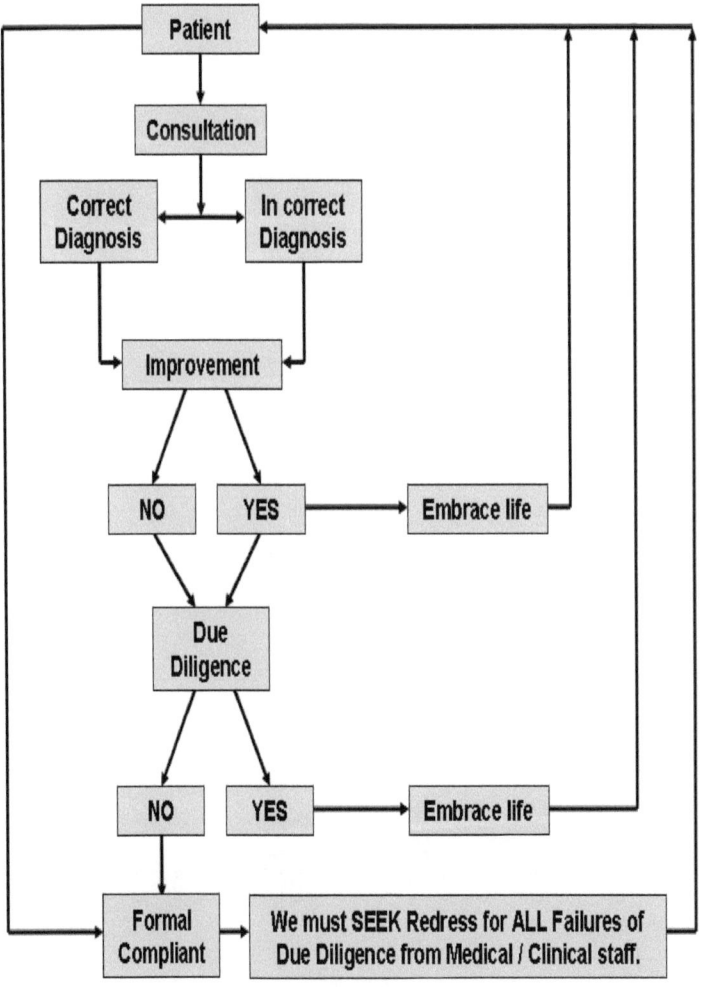

I have the power in me to be all that I was born to be and now I believe it !

I am a mortal living amongst mortals and I too have rights and needs

(6) FINDING THE ANSWERS

It's fair to say that some of us really go through the mill several times before our illness is finally diagnosed, yet at the point we're diagnosed we then hopefully via an effective treatment regime, can begin to make a substantive recovery from our presenting conditions. Sadly however, some of us actually never recover and that's primarily due to two reasons:

- Our condition is terminal.

- Or analytical sciences and clinical investigations are simply unable to detect a problem.

Ironically, during my baron chronic illness resolution days, whilst I was failed wholesale by UK analytical sciences and clinical investigations, I was diagnosed as terminally ill in the USA. How strange is that?

Well not that strange really when you scratch the surface of analytical sciences and clinical investigations in the UK. You see, the vast majority of tests, machines, and imaging devices that we have in the UK are not state of the art as the industry or our government would like us to believe. They're actually state of the ark. It's not until you actually analyse the state of that medical service sector that you find out just how bad things really are.

I have the power in me to be all that I was born to be and now I believe it !

A situation compounded further by the front end medical cretins who request investigations and then either play a part or choose to abstain from interpolating any subsequent results objectively leaving us as the sufferer bemused.

I really don't think there can be anything worse than having a major health impediment and yet because of out dated and fundamentally flawed analytical sciences and clinical investigations no one can find anything wrong with you. At that point despite your intense suffering you're simply written off as a neurotic and the most alarming thing is that there is no difference either between the NHS and the private sector.

Time after time I've paid for very expensive consultations and tests and time after time some pompous, greedy, ignorant 'medical rogue' has said to me, 'actually there's nothing wrong with you your tests are normal Mr. Hardy' Followed by, 'have you considered psychiatric help?'

Equally in the NHS I've been abused in far too many situations by 'medical rogues' saying, 'Mr. Hardy there's absolutely nothing wrong with you it's all in your head' and their other favourite line, 'Mr. Hardy we can't keep on testing you why can't you just accept that you have a mental health issue?'

It is primarily because of all the rubbish and abuse I've had to endure that I advocate that we must take control of this situation. How dare some talentless, badly trained yet public sector worker say that the NHS can't keep testing me or anyone of us? I've / we've funded their bloody training, I / we've funded their bloody life styles and some of us have battled to preserve their bloody rotten industry from the ravages of Thatcherism. Boy do those 'charlatans' really make me angry.

I am a mortal living amongst mortals and I too have rights and needs

You see, I really don't give a hoot if the NHS has to perform a thousand bloody tests upon me to find out what's wrong with me, that's what it's there for and therefore that's what it needs to do. Or it could certainly begin in the name of greater efficiencies, to look at the amount of money it's wasting on fundamentally flawed analytical sciences and clinical investigations and start bring its house in order.

Because if some clerical or 'clinical rogue' is assigning limits to the level of care that I can have from the NHS, then I for one now say let's have voluntary contributions to the NHS. Why should I a potential high earner pay ridiculous amounts of money to underwrite an industry that doesn't want to underwrite me when I need it? Yet it throws billions away on consultant's salaries and treats any chancer who decides to pop over to the UK for treatment.

Now hey I would never in a million years have thought that this working class lad from Woodhouse would ever have held such views towards the NHS. But having been exposed head on to all its woeful underperformance, ignorance and incompetence for years, I'm happy to voice my harsh views now. My belief now is that we need to bring this entire rotten industry crashing to its knees. So that as a nation we're able to build a clinical care service sector that is thorough, competitive; inspirational and world class and let's ditch the clap trap and rubbish of the past.

I have the power in me to be all that I was born to be and now I believe it !

The problem with that vision is that the people who have suffered most from its shoddy service are unfortunately the ones with the lowest vitality, presence or voice. So before any of its victims can commit to campaigning for change they need to get well for only then can they hope to bring about change. But be under no illusion that dynamic changes quickly at the point our health returns. Unfortunately the road to recovery can be lonely, long and unrewarding at times and so until we reach our desired destination, its best for all chronically ill patients to focus solely upon regaining their health and leave the clinical reform campaign to better times.

Prior to our return to health however, let me give you a flavour of what happens in the normal psyche when we're experiencing a health condition and require analytical sciences and/or clinical investigations. We immediately make either a big or small deal of the fact that our condition is going to be subject to further scrutiny. Some of us may be worried that something dreadful may be found, whilst others may simply be happy if something could be found to enable us to be treated, recover and move on. I've always come from the school of thought, 'I hope they can find something so that I could move on'. I've never subscribed to worrying about there being something dreadfully wrong with me, because I only ever wanted solutions. I knew for years that I had something seriously wrong with me; I just didn't know what it was. If we don't know what's wrong with us then we can't ever hope to recover and in poor health, recovery must be our sole interest if we wish to regain some form of quality of life. Therefore we must commit to testing and analytical investigations and when the results come through, we must do our level best to acknowledge them and deal with them as appropriately as we're able to or at the very least, see fit.

I am a mortal living amongst mortals and I too have rights and needs

So let's play the cycle through now, our test results come back and they're always in the standard form of:

- (a) Your tests are normal.

- (b) Hmmn, there is a slight problem but that might just be congenital.

- (c) You have bla bla bla bla.

- (d) You need to make an appointment to discuss your results.

Now to understand the ramifications of that feedback we need to look at the two generic psyches I discussed earlier i.e. big or small deal propensity. So let's look at the big deal psyche first:

(a) Results normal = maybe happy deep down and prepared to take whatever the medical representative says in terms of treatments etc., but may ham it up a bit when speaking to colleagues, family and friends.

(b) Result might be a congenital issue = may be worried deep down yet prepared to take whatever the medical representative says in terms of treatments etc. Might however blow the condition completely out of proportion and will certainly ham it up a bit when speaking to colleagues, family and friends.

(c) Result you have bla bla = may be extremely worried and also might blow the condition completely out of proportion until reassured by the medic, but will certainly ham it up a lot when speaking to colleagues, family and friends.

I have the power in me to be all that I was born to be and now I believe it !

(d) Result you need a follow up appointment = extremely worried and will blow the condition completely out of proportion, because that brings the drama they crave into their life. As long as it's a safe and controllable drama that's fine, should it however not be a safe drama then they will start off being publicly very brave and then simply implode putting tremendous pressure on anyone in close proximity.

So let's look at the small deal psyche now:

(a) Results normal = maybe confused deep down but prepared to take to some extent whatever the medical representative says.

(b) Result might be a congenital issue = may be worried but certainly interested in the result more from a clinical perspective than a sensationalist perspective.

(c) Result you have bla bla = may be worried but happy that there is something to discuss, but will need answers.

(d) Result you need a follow up appointment = worried until they understand what's wrong with them, but once they know they just get their heads down with it and are normally stronger than the people around them, who sometimes fall to pieces.

Now look it doesn't really matter what personality type you fall into. The key to returning to optimum health is ensuring that you're either prepared to be driven or you're prepared to drive the situation. Either way your focus must be upon achieving optimum health, because if you're not experiencing optimum health then you need to understand why; assuming that is that optimum health is your real goal. I've postulated that we must all examine if optimum health is our real goal, and I raise that challenging point because whilst some people will say optimum health is their goal. You only have to talk or listen to them to understand that they are indeed lost or closed to the potential of optimum health. That is because some people really do like being ill, because in being ill they:

- Have the crutch they need.

- Don't need to compete.

- Can offload all their personal issues at the door of their illness or disease.

I have the power in me to be all that I was born to be and now I believe it !

Now there is absolutely no crime in that, save to say, if a man does not wish to help himself, then perhaps help is not what he needs. You see there are no secrets to optimum health save for a desire to have optimum health, yet within that expectation and desire there are many levels of acceptance and abstinence. Only we as individuals have the sole right to make the value judgments that best meet our desires and needs.

My personal expectations have always been to secure a quality of life that is free from physical impediments and diseased states. Because of that I've mapped a holistic yet pragmatic approach to this process on the next page, now whilst it may initially look complex when you first see it. Just take time to follow some of the evolution and iteration loops from your own perspective and you'll find that it caters precisely for whichever mind set you are.

I am a mortal living amongst mortals and I too have rights and needs

Surviving The Great Medical Care Swindle

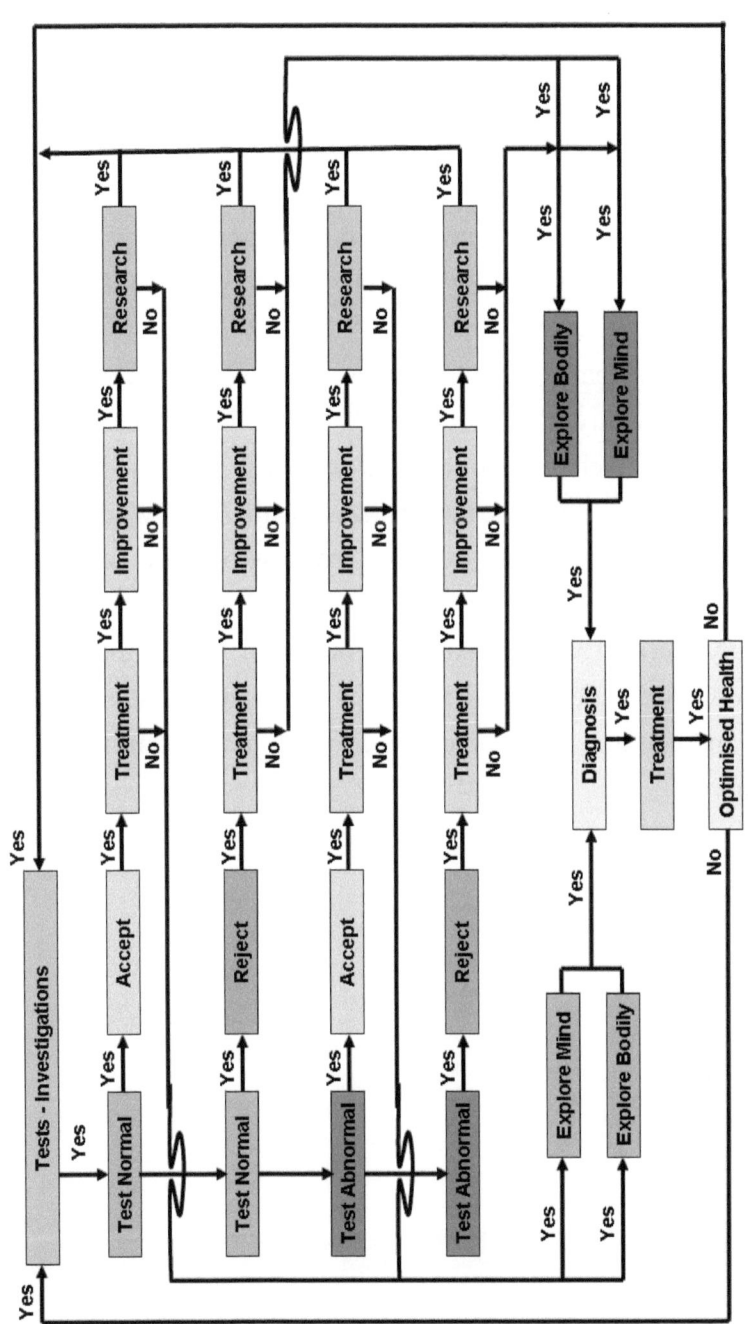

The only secret to having good health is ones personal determination to have good health

I have the power in me to be all that I was born to be and now I believe it !

During my pre-diagnostic state my only abstinences were to reject wholesale any and all forms of clap trap or ignorantly manufactured dogma articulated to distract me from my goal. I advocate only this that in the pursuit of optimum health we all must accept that we alone are the responsible party for driving the process of recovery through diagnosis. For without our input, there is no other form of input worthy of comment and therefore no reasonable probability of making any form of sustainable recovery.

Yet whilst that is, or can be, a very difficult path for some of us to walk alone, in reality it's the only path that delivers access to clarity, understanding, effective treatment and recovery. It is by default however; a process of two stages, the first stage is the stage where we are in essence ignorant and unable to make progress because we rely completely upon false testing, consultations and investigations which have little if any merit. I've mapped that process for you on the next page, because once we understand all the loops in the process, it is no longer a mystery and can indeed become that defining point from which we all move forward.

I am a mortal living amongst mortals and I too have rights and needs

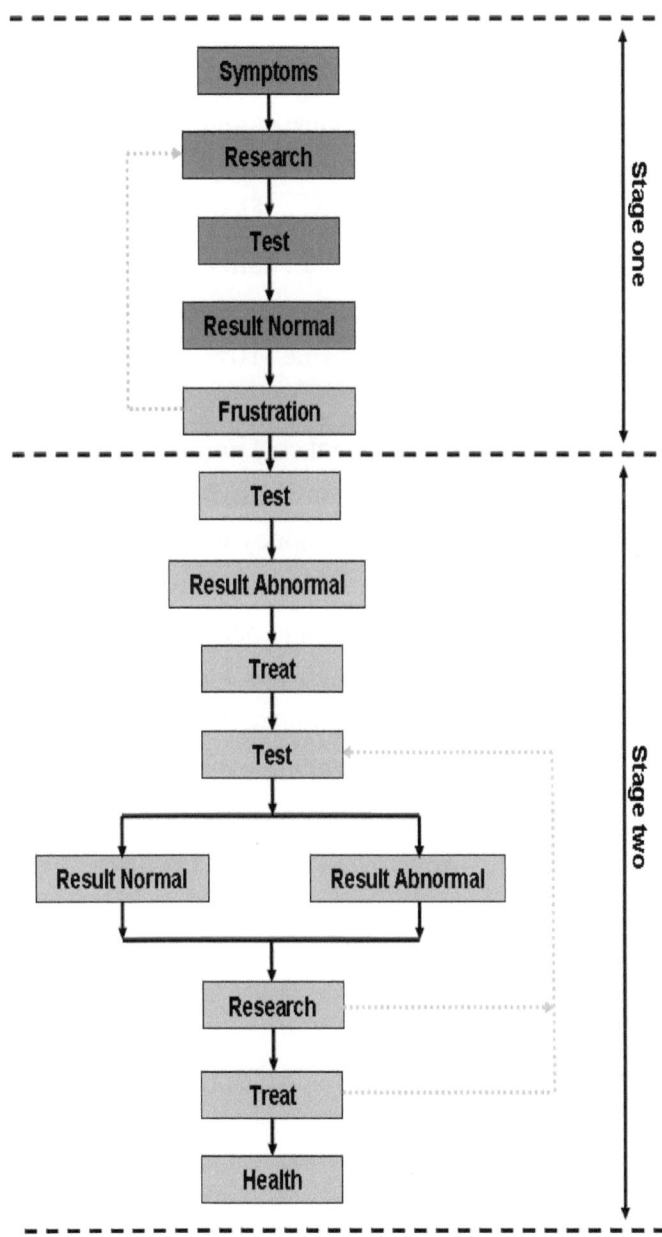

Ignore the doubters who say you can't keep on testing you can and you must

I have the power in me to be all that I was born to be and now I believe it !

The second stage is where we take ownership of the intellect responsibility for substantiating our underlying condition or conditions. It is the point that we start unravelling our health mysteries, that remarkable point where we see the medical industry and those who support it for what and who they really are.

Both stages are incredibly difficult because they are both encountered when we have lower than normal vitality. Stage one will invariably consist of a 90% - 10% NHS and private involvement whereas 'stage two' will be the complete opposite i.e. 10% - 90% NHS and private involvement.

Therefore there are significant cost implications required of those attempting to return to a position of optimum health. Some of that money will be wasted and some of it will be money well spent. There is no right or wrong course of action to take, all we can ever be is true to ourselves and whilst we can't beat the obscene and perverse nature of the medical industry. We can get better through our own efforts and eventually realise our dreams if only we're prepared to drive the testing and analysis until a reflective diagnosis has been achieved. In my particular situation stage one of my investigation process consisted of nothing more than the following fundamentally flawed investigations below:

- 3 Liver enzyme tests.

- 3 Thyroid tests.

- 1 MRI.

- 1 CT.

- 1 X-ray investigation.

I am a mortal living amongst mortals and I too have rights and needs

The conclusions drawn from them were that I was fine and had nothing wrong with me except for mental health issues, time and time again. Whereas my stage two self funded investigations included:

- 5 MRI's.
- 2 MRA's.
- 4 CAT scans.
- 2 CT's.
- 60+ blood tests and bodily function analysis, tests and examinations.
- 9 Caloric Tests.
- 3 Hearing Tests.
- 9 ENG Tests.
- Two Neurosurgical procedures.
- 180+ clinical consultations all around the world plus travel and accommodation.
- Plus thousands of hours research on the internet long before cheap broad band, etc.
- In summation personal traceable costs in excess of 300K.

I have the power in me to be all that I was born to be and now I believe it !

The result of my tenacity in the face of unbelievable odds was that I was eventually diagnosed with:

- Chronic late stage Lymes Disease.

- Chronic mitochondria failure.

- Chronic liver disease.

- Chronic adrenal insufficiency.

- And an extremely rare genetic yet organic anomaly resulting in a Posterior Inferior Cerebella Artery insulting my vestibular bundle and brain stem left side. *Note this condition still imposes great suffering upon me every minute of every day and that's why just putting my thoughts onto paper is such an almighty affair.*

Now look, the point I'm making is that there are far too many issues surrounding our poor medical investigation model and too many issues surrounding outdated machines and devices being postulated as state of the art diagnostic tools. How many of us actually know until we are faced with horrendous medical conditions just how bad the equipment and techniques used to analyse our bodies truly are through-out the nhs because if we did I'm sure our own dogs of war would be unleashed.

How many of us have been for an MRI scan and been told that everything is normal, when in reality the MRI scanner being used is:

- Badly designed and maintained?

- Outdated and malfunctioning?

- An expensive piece of scrap metal?

- Operated by people who don't give a shit.

Now we all know the difference between top and low end motoring in terms of performance etc, but very few of us know that the same is the case in the medical industry. You see, in the push to kid us all into thinking our health is safe in their hands, NHS trusts all around the country installed sub standard equipment which in the majority of instances are nothing more than token gestures in terms of world class clinical investigation tools. The differences are so wide in terms of performing basic functions that it's like giving one man a set of binoculars and another an electron microscope to analyse the same bacteria, now that would be simply ridiculous wouldn't it?

Well the truth is, the state of our nation's clinical diagnostic tools is not simply ridiculous, it's actually a disgrace and we the front end users or mugs are the ones paying the highest price. We're sent for diagnostic investigations, the results come back normal and the result of that is, no further line of investigation undertaken despite the fact that your condition may continue to decline.

I have the power in me to be all that I was born to be and now I believe it !

Simply because a shit piece of equipment operated by people who don't give a shit has indicating that you have no problem or in point of fact is unable to detect the problem you have. Now I sincerely hope that my observations through suffering and personal wasted expense has set off some alarm bells deep within you because those alarm bells need to resonate with us all as a society each and every day because we need this resolved not next year or next month I would respectfully suggest but tomorrow and it must happen before lunch time at the very latest.

Because I advocate that when and where there is evidence to suggest that the instruments, techniques, systems and protocols used to support clinical investigations are incapable of investigating with the degree of enquiry that we need, then we need to:

- Challenge the results.

- Find suitable systems etc, which can perform to the level and standard of integrity that we require.

You see, I'm no solo foot soldier here, millions of us are being written off every year by fundamentally flawed medical investigations, consultations and tests. So if you truly desire optimum health, you're going to have to fight for it with all your intellect, strength and might. You're going to have to:

- Ignore the personal and clinical prejudices that you encounter.

- You're going to have to spend money that you may not have.

- You're going to have to prove your condition yourself.

I am a mortal living amongst mortals and I too have rights and needs

Because if you think for one moment that the state, the NHS or our private medical health circus will resolve anything more than a superficial health impediment then your sadly mistaken because they won't. Only you can drive this stage two part of your pursuit of disease expression reflective diagnosis, because in reality there really only is you who truly gives a damn. So to help keep you upbeat and focused during that process I've mapped a very simple process approach plan for you below.

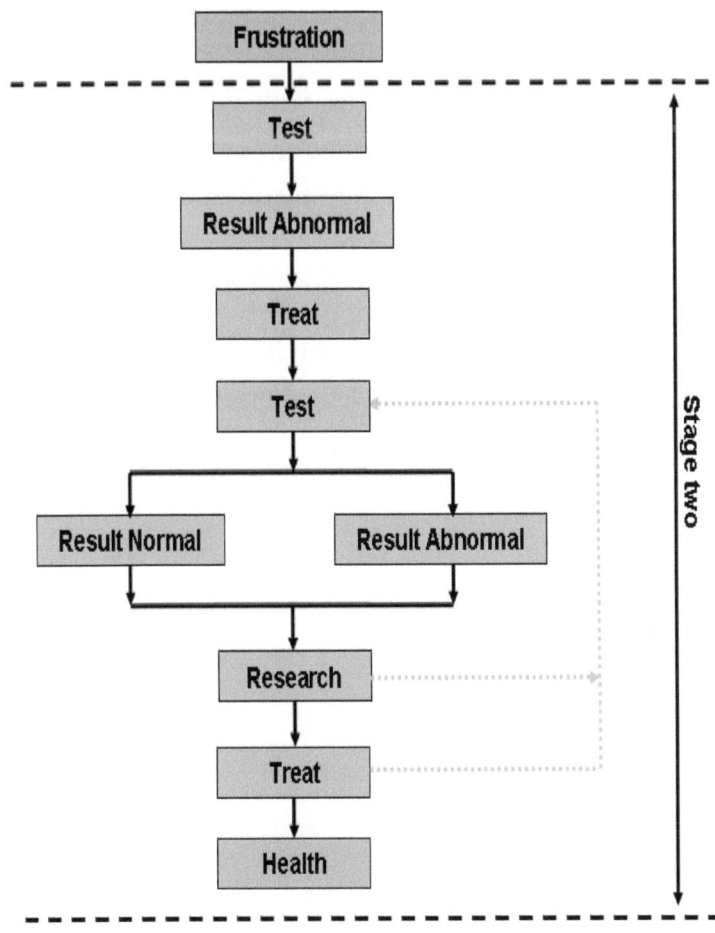

Ignore the doubters who say you can't keep on testing you can and you must

I have the power in me to be all that I was born to be and now I believe it !

So that when you're at the other end of your health recovery campaign you can then speak from a platform of assurance, confidence and righteousness. You can challenge the integrity of those who failed you, ignored or abused you, because at that point you're more than an equal for anyone who would choose to play games with you because you're able to ask with assurance:

- Why are we as a nation wasting so much money on fundamentally flawed tests etc., whilst writing people off with impunity?

- Why are some of us, with a desire to be well, having to self research, self fund and self acquire best in class medical and clinical investigations outside the UK?

- Where is the medical establishment when we need it?

- Who within our current appalling medical service sector ranks can dare to defend this level of clinical and administrated incompetence?

I am a mortal living amongst mortals and I too have rights and needs

There really is only one way to ensure that you get through your health predicaments and that is to take control of your stage two process whilst ensuring you stay in total control of your entire health optimisation process re: below.

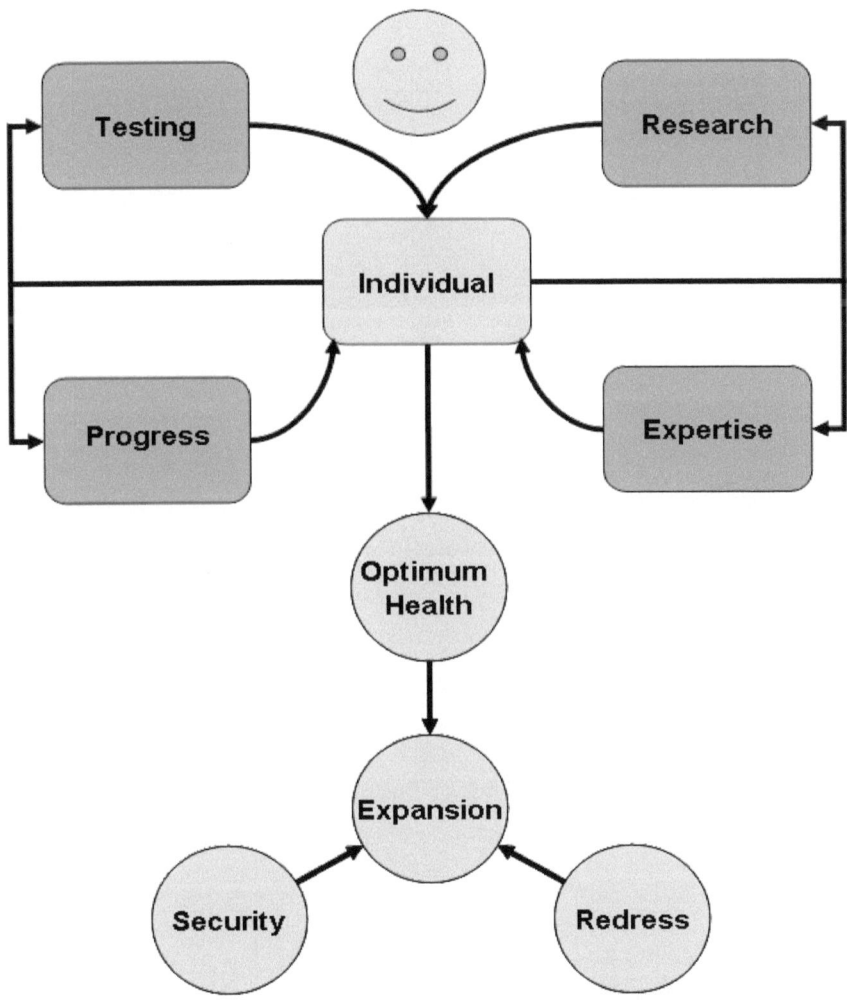

Taking Individual Control of All Health Related Processes

I have the power in me to be all that I was born to be and now I believe it !

I am a mortal living amongst mortals and I too have rights and needs

(7) A VERY PERSONAL BATTLE

Unless you've battled with something like an undiagnosed chronic health condition its difficult to understand just what extraordinary lengths we as mortals will go to just to find answers, treatment and/or rest. Believe me some of the lengths I went to looking back now are simply mind-blowing and if the majority of them hadn't been such dreadful experiences then they'd be considered hilarious, and that includes both orthodox and the not so orthodox approaches.

You know, you try to get answers from the medical industry, you try to find answers for yourself and you even try the best mystics you can find but there really are times when there are no answers to be had. That's when life becomes as lonely and terrible as mortality can possibly be. During my illness, I travelled tens of thousands of miles and I explained my symptoms and my case over and over again, in swanky clinics, gritty shit holes and even people's offices in garden sheds. During that time I got a lot of:

- Head nodding. ………
- Hmmn's………
- I see's……..

I have the power in me to be all that I was born to be and now I believe it !

What I never got was the one thing I was looking for, the answer to the illness that was crucifying me. I really don't know how I kept going at times, for even when I felt that it was the wrong thing to do or the wrong person to see, I did it and saw them just in case I was wrong and perhaps they would prove that to me. Time after time it was the same reply 'Hmmn Mr. Hardy your case is very complicated' to the extent that I've even said to some of them in the end:

- *'If you're even thinking of telling me that I've got a difficult case, you can stop right there. I know I've got a difficult case, that's why I'm here paying you a fortune just to sit there and nod your bloody head, if it was easy do you not think I would have solved it myself rather than coming here to see you, a so called bloody expert instead'.*

It's no wonder at times that some of them were rocked by my presence, but by that point I didn't give a hoot, I was weary of all of my conditions and even wearier of being turned over by money grabbing bandits and incompetent sods. Some of things I experienced were simply insane e.g.

1. I agreed in principle to pay one particular so called neurological expert an absolute fortune to be seen by him, his reply after the explanation of my case was; *'All I hear is words, but what is your problem?, you're talking about things that you can't possible have'*. I'd just sat and explained all my inter-cranial symptoms to the pompous bastard and he had the audacity to sit there in his third rate crumpled bloody grey suit and say that to me. I just looked him straight in the eye and said; *'Listen very carefully to me pal, if you're trying to play psychological games with me be very careful, because I don't play games when its much more satisfying simply to break the bloody neck of arseholes like you'*. The guy at that point got all flustered and immediately started to back track, but I just said; *'Yo dude; you can stop right there, this meeting is over! And don't even think of charging me for this rubbish because you wouldn't like it if I for any reason had to come back here to see you, okay?'*

I have the power in me to be all that I was born to be and now I believe it !

2. I somehow managed to drive over to Newcastle to see another so called professor of neurology and after he'd gone through the same bog standard gait and cerebella checks I'd had countless times in the past he announced; *'Well dear boy there's nothing wrong with you that a course of anti depressants wouldn't cure'.* To which my reply was, *'Hang on a minute you're a neurologist not a psychiatrist and what about the pressure inside my head?* There was a brief moment of silence and then he said, *'Come come dear boy, you don't have any pressure inside your head you're only suggesting that you have pressure inside your head'. 'Er……*no *I'm telling you I have pressure in my head so let me ask you this; what are you going to do to help take that away'.* His reply was, *'Nothing dear boy it's only a symptom it's not real you only think you have pressure inside your head'.* I was raging by now and not a little unwell so I said, *'Let me ask you this you fucking pompous fat twat, if I kick you in the balls which I'm very tempted to do right now, will you have a pain in your balls or just a symptom of pain in the balls?'* At which point the guy said; *'My word no one has ever spoken to me like that before'.* As I turned to leave the room, I looked back at him over my shoulder and said; *'Your luck has just run out dear boy,* **do not** *under any circumstance send me a bill for this fucking clap trap, okay dear boy?'*

I am a mortal living amongst mortals and I too have rights and needs

Now it sounds as if I didn't pay my way as I sought the help I needed, but nothing could be further from the point. I notched up outrageous debts paying people who were supposed to be helping me, who were in reality only lining their own greedy pockets as I continued to suffer.

Like most processes however, there is a point of change, and I'd reached that point of change, I was extremely tired of living and I wasn't prepared to have my last few pounds mugged from me by some toffee nosed rogue filling his pockets on a Saturday morning on premises belonging to the NHS at my expense.

Nevertheless as I've said we'll try anything when we're desperate enough and I was desperate enough indeed so I even tried North American Drum therapy of all things with a head which felt fit to explode at one point. The therapy was conducted in the back room of a very lentils and beads charlatan, who went into great depth in terms of explaining to me just how good she was and then she danced around me banging a drum above my head for the best part of 30 minutes shouting out; *'Be gone dark energy be gone'*.

Well there was no change when she'd finished as I'm sure you're highly amused to discover, but in my despair I arranged to have four further treatments in the coming days of that week at £45 a session. However when I arrived for the final session I could tell she was all stressed out and she said she thought she was about to go down with a migraine because her boiler pilot light had just gone out and she couldn't get it back on.

I have the power in me to be all that I was born to be and now I believe it !

Can you believe that? My head was fit to explode with chronic Lymes Disease and yet I was paying some chancer £45 to bang a drum above my head to apparently clear away bad energy and yet she can't cope because of all things the pilot light on her boiler had just gone out? I just looked at her, smiled and said, *'Now that's very interesting my headache is still the same as its been for years but my pilot light has just this minute come back on and that's telling me that you're nothing but the charlatan that I've suspected you were all along'.*

She just looked at me gormlessly as I turned, put my jacket back on and headed for the door, she shouted out *'But but'* I just replied *'bang your drum pet for 5 or 10 minutes and I'm sure your headache will have gone by then and when it has give me a call and for £135 I'll give you the number of a very very good plumber who'll sort that pilot light out for you no bother'.*

All highly amusing hey, my west cumbrian repartee with the pompous git and the drum banging fraud? Well in reality it's not at all funny, because when we're in a state of desperation I personally think it's a disgrace that the world appears to be full of shits just sitting and waiting to rob us of our money. Nevertheless and as a sanity check I fully accept that during my life that I've been tortured and let down by my body in many ways that it's impossible to comprehend. But if I think about all the qualities I personally possess, the one that gives me the greats joy of all is not my passion, drive or tenacity in the face of incredulous odds, it's actually my incredible sense of humour which remains ever present even to this day.

I am a mortal living amongst mortals and I too have rights and needs

Sometimes it's not at all easy to laugh at life or indeed laugh at ourselves and the situations or predicaments that we often find ourselves in. But if we can laugh at our own absurdity even for moment in the face of incredible or intense adversity, then I truly believe that we have a better chance of re-energizing ourselves because laughter always but always brings along with it almost instantaneous and momentary relief.

I have the power in me to be all that I was born to be and now I believe it !

Moving on, I think perhaps the most perverse issue that I became aware of whilst I desperately sought help from the medical/clinical industry was the: 'Dear Sir, I wonder if you would kindly see this man' and the; 'Dear Sir thank you for asking me to see this man' bloody medical/clinical bullocks and clap trap communiqués. Such was my great annoyance with this shit that I sort of created my own acronym after a while, *Dear Sir Bollocks Letters*, DSBL's. If you've ever experienced this crap you'll know what I mean i.e. 'Dear Sir I wrote several letters on your behalf but apparently you had the affront to die without informing me, please note my bill for £350.00 is enclosed, payment conditions strictly within14 days'.

It's simply outrageous what goes on in the medical/clinical world, they spend more time putting together or dictating implicitly incorrect bullshit communiqués than they actually spend seeing or treating people either directly or indirectly in their care. Equally you can wait months to see a so called expert, but when you arrive for your appointment you find that it's not the expert who's going to see you now, it's some bloody registrar who's clueless and nervous about everything. These people are playing with people's lives and yet they simply don't get it. You attend these NHS or rip off private consultations and then you read the reply correspondence some weeks later that you've been CC'd into and it's like what is this idiot on about? I didn't say any of that!

What's even more hilarious is that there's never even a hint of a positive suggestion or any form of potential resolution forthcoming from these communiqués, but there is always the obligatory reference to conjunctive counselling etc.

I am a mortal living amongst mortals and I too have rights and needs

It really is a scandal, people are dying whilst these rogues write DSBL's to each other, letters that make no sense, letters that corrupt your files, letters for the sake of writing bloody letters. These people are a complete waste of space and an affront to everything decent. But it's worse than that, I remember seeing a so called expert on the south coast about my vestibular condition who then wrote a DSBL to my private GP. Suggesting that even though she was an expert in her field of medicine, it would perhaps is better if a saw someone whom she felt was more of an expert than her. Now hey some might read that and think 'hmmn very laudable' wrong, wrong, wrong, wrong, wrong. This person makes a living as a so called expert in her clinical field, so why couldn't she just pick up the phone and discuss my case with this other so called experts? Well because:

- (a) She didn't give a hoot about me or my suffering.

And

- (b) It was an opportunity for her to send some cash the way of one of her buddies, which is simply sickening really.

I have the power in me to be all that I was born to be and now I believe it !

But wait, it gets better; she finished her communiqué by saying whilst she was uncertain about the origin of my condition she would respectfully suggest that there was more than enough evidence to suggest that my condition could be more of psychological condition and not simply of organic origin. Brilliant eh? *'We are all experts but some of us are far more of an expert than others, and those of us who are not as expert as we think we are, can make if we choose too; expert assumptions about the origins of disease from a clinical perspective that we're not even qualified in, let alone expert enough to understand'.*

Sorry but there's more, when she sent her invoice out to me, there on the bottom of her invoice for £200 in bold was, *Note receipts will only be provided upon the forwarding of a stamp addressed envelope.* I really was tired of rogues like this by now so I personally wrote a DSBL back to her and advised her that I wouldn't be providing a stamp addressed envelope. Indeed I advised her that if she wished payment from me she would need to rethink her greed strategy quickly because I was certainly thinking of submitting her invoice to Trading Standards for closer scrutiny. The matter of my receipt was resolved quickly but I still submitted her invoice to the Trading Standards, screw her, the greedy, nasty, ignorant, pompous charlatan.

I am a mortal living amongst mortals and I too have rights and needs

In another instance I had a private consultation in the north east with a little runt of a man, who conducted my entire private consultation with his door wide open. Time after time he just let rip into me and shouted at me as if I were a dog. It was the worst consultation I'd ever had and I remember coming out and being completely shell shocked by the whole thing. Within two or three days his invoice came and I thought screw you, I wrote out his cheque and attached it to a CC'd letter that I sent to the NHS trust where he was practicing making a formal complaint about his unacceptable conduct. Four days later the cheque was returned by his PA with a covering letter stating, in light of my dissatisfaction with the consultation, he'd decided not to charge me. I was very tempted to bill the poisoned dwarf for my travel expenses but I thought sod it, he's admitted liability for his impropriety, I have his DSBL on record and that was good enough for me.

I have the power in me to be all that I was born to be and now I believe it !

Around that time I had my second private MRI of the brain, and after six weeks I contacted the office of the consultant I'd seen to enquire where my results were. After days and days going around and around in circles they apparently managed to find my information but as yet he hadn't had time to analyse my results.

Can you believe that I'd paid £1150 for a private consultation and MRI and the so called highly recommended private clinician hadn't even looked at my films seven weeks after they'd been taken? A further two weeks after that I received a call from a very snotty clinical secretary saying, *'Nothing to worry about I had a watery cyst the size of a plum bottom left side of my brain but it had been concluded that it was a congenital condition and nothing to do with my presenting symptoms'*. My reply was; *'Well it wasn't on my last MRI'* to which her reply was, *'I can't comment on that you will need to speak to Mr. bla bla when he returns back from his six month sabbatical'*.

I was beginning to discover that there were no health workers with any decency, integrity, sensitivity or technical competence i.e. they don't give a hoot about anyone in their care and if a medic can't understand or doesn't know what a presenting image or symptom is than the best way to deal with it is to write it off as congenital.

What's simply staggering about this situation is that eighteen month later after extensive Lymes Disease treatment I asked during my third private MRI results discussion about the cyst. The guy just looked at me and said, *'What cyst'* to which I replied; *'The plum sized cyst bottom left side of my brain'*. His reply was, *'Oh that area there, it's probably nothing more than congenital discolouration nothing to be concerned about'*. I said;

I am a mortal living amongst mortals and I too have rights and needs

'No no there was a cyst there eighteen months ago' to which he replied with utter contempt, *'If you say so but I'm telling you there's no evidence to suggest there was a cyst there in fact there's nothing wrong with you that perhaps some yoga, counselling or antidepressants wouldn't sort out'.*

How dare those fucking bastards think they can do and say what they like to us. Well they can I'm afraid to say simply because they're proactively encouraged to engage in such despicable conduct by their industrial luddite peers.

What's more and I have to say however, that some of the biggest jokers I ever saw where those 'clowns and deviants' that populate Harley Street, in total I saw 14 of them at a cost of over 9k for consultations, tests and MRI's etc. Never have I ever met such highly inflated egos working within an industry who are as fraudulent in all their dealings as the greedy, incompetent medical charlatans who buy themselves into the cash rich cows or rooms as they like to call them on Harley Street.

These people are the biggest rogues any mortal is ever likely to meet; they are all without exception, completely up their own arseholes and lacking in any form of human decency. I completely refuse to see them as anything other than they what are, the worst form of all mortal life forms, rogues masquerading as healers whilst lining their pocket through greed.

My advice these days to anyone suffering from a chronic condition is; do NOT go anyway near Harley Street, save your money and seek out true clinical excellence in Europe or any other part of the developed world. But please stay well clear of those horrible greedy fucking slime balls that prostitute their services in said locality.

I have the power in me to be all that I was born to be and now I believe it !

Now look, I couldn't possible go into all the things I encountered during my desperate, desperate years and don't think you would wish to read them anyway. What I will state is that it is safe to say that when we are ill or when we are desperate enough, nothing is beyond or should be beyond our explorations in search of wellness. The only points that I would make are; tread gently and pay no one who's opening line is I'm promising nothing.

You see; I've met hundreds of those charlatans and each and everyone them has mugged me with a smile of their face. My illness has changed me in so many ways, I've never liked bull-shitters or rogues and whilst I could sort of live with them before my illness. Today I'm extremely comfortable enough with myself to tell someone their talking bollocks if I think they are e.g. if I were to go to an Italian restaurant and ask the chef *'how good he/she was at preparing sea food linguini?'* and he or she replied, *'not bad but I'm making no promises'*. I would immediately think, *'Fuck that for a game of soldiers and tell him/her exactly what I thought of their reply and then leave to find a restaurant and chef who knew what the fuck they were doing'*.

Similarly we must take that approach when interacting with so called health workers. Because there are far too many rogues out there, making a living at the expense of people with chronic conditions in both orthodox and non orthodox applications. In fact the horrible bastards are everywhere these days. They charge you for your time as you give them your case history and they charge for all the materials they use on top of everything else, nothing is free and all you're ever seen as is; a simpleton or cash cow to them. Their favourite line is, 'Give it some time' when things for you are not getting any better.

I am a mortal living amongst mortals and I too have rights and needs

But they never ever say, 'Look, I'm really sorry, but I'm not charging you anything for this appointment, because I haven't got a clue what's wrong with you and furthermore I don't know anyone whom I can recommend that you should see'. The plain fact of this unsavoury side of illness is that healers simply don't heal people, what they do is earn money and support livelihoods at the expense of the chronically ill. You will know if your healer is any good or not because your body will be the first to let you know.

Now this might sound strange or insane but believe me its true, the greatest and most powerful healer of all is the healer that resides deep within us. Let us never forget that, we can always heal ourselves if we choose to live our life with that sense of inner personal belief, all we need is the inner strength at times of low vitality to enable us to find the answers that we need. In a chronic illness state, no one is going to take sympathy upon you and give of their expertise for free, very few will be kind to you or have your best interests at heart.

The way to look at healers is no different from any other form of practitioner; they have a set of skills which they're charging you for on the open market, they are certainly doing you no favours. Therefore chronic ill health costs money and generates great income, so don't ever forget that it's a business not a moral or social service or responsibility.

Above all things, take care, and may you understand when you're in the presence of greatness our merely interacting with 'clowns' for the difference in service delivery should be immediately evident in your healers deeds and not in any bullshitting words or phrase that they may wish to cite or use.

I have the power in me to be all that I was born to be and now I believe it !

At my age now and with all my terrible experiences it's easy for me to lament upon that fact that life is certainly a very real and gigantic challenge for some of us complicated by default by the sheer volume of clinical/medical charlatans, idiots, slime balls, cretins and clowns that we unfortunately have to meet.

All I can say on that point is let's bring back capital punishment, and let's start hanging, beheading and flogging a medic every day 'again' until our message finally gets through their incredulous, think, insensitive and callus skins that we want;

- Accountability

- Decency

And

- Excellent from them in all their undertakings because that is not an aspiration in any way shape of form, it's actually a real and a deservedly righteous expectation.

(8) Treatments options

It was during the worst points in my illness when I discovered that orthodox medical clinicians seemed to be amongst the most technically ignorant so called professionals I'd ever encountered in my life. Nevertheless, there are some men and women of science on the fringe of that industry trying their level best to help people and to move the science of medicine along from the middle age culture that it remains to this day stuck in. The problem those guys face is that they are trying to change a culture that simply doesn't want to change. A position which invariably means that they are immediately referred to as quacks by their luddite medical peers, which means that being treated by them can become so much more difficult that it needs to be or should be.

Now hey I'm not saying that all pioneering clinicians are good guys because some are clearly not. I do however find it incredibly annoying to listen to incompetent orthodox clinicians rubbishing and or trying to dig dirt on people who are clinically committed to moving things forward. Whilst they themselves are responsible on a grandiose scale for legitimised medical genocide of the majority of people entrusted into their care. It is this macrobiotic and immutability of the medical industry that is really holding clinical treatment progress back. You see; here is an endemic culture of assumption within the medical industry

I have the power in me to be all that I was born to be and now I believe it !

which on the one hand prescribes as it sees fit, whilst on the other simply attacks and criticizes alternative approaches, based upon nothing than prejudices or personal understandings or assumptions. In the absence of clinical data they will cry foul, yet in the presence of flawed historical orthodox clinical data they will defend it to the hilt.

You only have to listen to, speak to, or be spoken to by an individual from the medical industry to appreciate just how technically incompetent they can be. How full of their own self importance they are and how intransigent they are to change and new ideas. Therefore is it any wonder then that the average clinician is reluctant to engage with new ideas, for to do so would immediately subject them to a level of scrutiny from their peers that they're simply not moralistically or intellectually able to defend?

It's for that reason and that reason only that we, as chronically ill people, must accept that when we engage in clinical dialogue with pioneers in the old fields of medical science, that both we and they are going to be ridiculed by any luddite we encounter along the way.

I am a mortal living amongst mortals and I too have rights and needs

You see, medical pioneering history is littered with victims of the systemically hypocritical and undoubtedly fear based corrupt judicial medical culture that appears to be hell bent upon stifling innovation. Where a preoccupation with the intentions, integrities and intellects of pioneering individuals have been brought into question and careers have been wrecked simply because some deviants are hell-bent on preventing clinical progression. Yet in far too many instances perhaps even after the pioneers' death the validity of what they were saying is later and often proven to be true.

I would therefore suggest that there has to be something fundamentally wrong with this industry and our society when:

- A clinician trying to move the envelope of medical science and clinical care forward has a proportionally greater chance of being medically disciplined or struck off, than some incompetent practitioner who's well known by his peers as being negligent in all that he or she does.

You see, I have nothing but praise for the clinical practitioners that I've met who:

- Listen.

- Treat holistically.

- Are prepared to explore new ways of being.

I have the power in me to be all that I was born to be and now I believe it !

You see; it's that approach and those sorts of people who will eventually change the lot of mankind for the better. Not the bullshitting cretins we encounter through our TV's or the pompous, arrogant, nasty, vindictive and incompetent rogues that we visit when we're in a state of disease. My chronic illness and the complete lack of clinical support at my disposal meant that I was forced to explore and self-fund many treatment protocols. That's why I feel it's only right that I document one or two of the treatments I explored if only to stimulate thought.

I am a mortal living amongst mortals and I too have rights and needs

Pyrrole Disorder

Prior to my Lymes Disease diagnosis, I make no secret of the fact that I've suffered from chronic suicidal depression and suggest that there can't possibly be anything worse than depression when absolutely nothing helps to remove or suppress its symptoms. Such was my physiological and emotional despair that I felt I needed to explore Pyroluria, a genetic condition that exhibits a wide range of symptoms most of which I'd had in the past or was suffering from at the time I explored this condition including:

- Episode of psychosis and suicidal depression.
- Little or no dream recall.
- White spots on finger nails.
- Poor morning appetite +/- tendency to skip breakfast.
- Morning nausea.
- Pale skin +/- poor tanning +/- burn easy in sun.
- Sensitivity to bright light.
- Hypersensitive to loud noises.
- Reading difficulties (e.g. dyslexia).
- Poor ability to cope with stress.
- Mood swings or temper outbursts.

I have the power in me to be all that I was born to be and now I believe it !

- Histrionic (dramatic).
- Argumentative/enjoy argument.
- Higher capability & alertness in the evening.
- Poor short term memory.
- Abnormal body fat distribution.
- Dry skin.
- Anxiousness.
- Significant growth after the age of sixteen.

Originally Pyroluria was known as malvaria which is a genetic abnormality in heamoglobin synthesis resulting in a deficiency of zinc and vitamin B6. People with pyroluria produce excess amounts of a by-product from hemoglobin synthesis, called OHHPL (hydroxyhemop pyrrolin-2-one). In these people an excess amount of pyrrole is found in the urine. Associated changes in fatty acid metabolism lead to low levels of arachidonicacid *an omega-6 fatty acid.* The presence of pyroluria can have a profound effect on mental and physical health and was first discovered in relation to schizophrenia. Now that's the science, here's the practicalities of the condition, you will not get tested or treated for Pyroluria on the NHS. You will need to test and pay privately via either hair or urine analysis should you decided to check for this condition. My only words of caution are that this condition is real and I tested positive for it, however;

I am a mortal living amongst mortals and I too have rights and needs

- Finding a responsive service provider is difficult; I lost my temper and composure completely with the slow turn around in my results i.e. 8 weeks which is completely unacceptable when we are in a chronic state of suicidal expression through disease.

- I've subsequently discovered issues with my body's methylation cycle which makes treating pyroluria complicated and although I didn't know it at the time it certainly explains why my treatment of pyroluria failed.

- Advocating my recovery theme that symptoms are nothing more than the presentation of disease, I think it's important to undergo more detailed investigation before attempting to treat or stabilise pyroluria symptoms.

I have the power in me to be all that I was born to be and now I believe it !

Exercise, yoga and meditation etc

Prior to my chronic health condition I was a highly active guy, running the high fells every weekend, whilst during the week comfortably running in excess of fifteen miles per day on the roads, cycling, weight training and all that after a hard day's work. One of the most important aspects of that regime was the mind and body work I completed after my physical exertion, because without relaxation and bodily cleansing I found my body simply didn't work or perform in a way that I expected of it and dare I say in my ignorance; demanded of it at times.

Yet some people never get this subtle recovery nuance, thinking that exercise in itself at whatever cost, is more than enough for a happy healthy life. However, if your body is in a diseased state or exhausted, then your bodily processes either slow down or give up the fight completely, at which point it's easy for all of us to lose all sense of quality in life. Therefore, whilst exercise and relaxation are essential components of optimum health, I would nevertheless suggest that those suffering from chronic illness exercise with extreme caution. Because when our body is in a diseased or a fatigued state it simply:

- Stops producing the products required to assist with bodily repair or toxin detoxification.

And

- Stops producing the energies we need to support the basic demands of living a normal healthy life.

Therefore, anything that puts either an unnecessary or greater strain on those processes is not helpful. In fact it could actually begin to compromise any effort you make to try to recover from your chronic health condition.

You see, our bodies must be able to recover from any physical load we place upon them no matter how gentle or therapeutic an activity is perceived e.g. yoga. A failure to understand this basic principle will leave you feeling constantly fatigued and ill, which is not in your long term recovery interests at all.

Therefore despite populist agendas which state that, when we're chronically ill, pursuit of activities such as yoga are actually good for us, as someone who's been chronically ill myself, I must and do fervently disagree. My personal experiences dictate that in the majority of instances exercise of any predisposition is counter-productive to healing at best and quite dangerous at worst, until our bodies have begun, through proactive intervention, the process of invigorated self-healing. I therefore would urge anyone suffering or recovering from a chronic illness NOT to explore physical exercise in any way shape or form until that is their body is well enough to deal with such demands.

I have the power in me to be all that I was born to be and now I believe it !

Vitamins & Amino Acids

I don't think there is a vitamin, mineral, amino acid, superfood, glandular, herb or supplement that I haven't taken in the past thirty years. Such has been my devotion to the pursuit of wellness that numerous health food shop owners have actually known me by my first name and have even asked me in many instances for feedback on the rarer products I've tried. I've shipped products to the UK from all around the world and yet I've never found one single product or associated treatment protocol that did what its hype postulated it was capable of doing.

Now there are many reasons for that, but the fact of the matter is that if we decided to take supplements, then we must be able to determine when they are working and when they are causing rebound side effects. I've had simply hundreds of harrowing experiences on my road to recovery but the one that sticks clearly in my mind is my desperate attempts to stabilise my depression by attempting to adhere to the key principles of the 'Mood Cure'.

The Mood Cure is a protocol which postulates a comprehensive natural approach to stabilising moods through the ingestion of amino acids combined with a high-protein, healthy-fat, veggie-rich diet and other nutritional strategies. The key component of this protocol being, a four-part questionnaire designed to identify your mood type, therein once qualified mapping an appropriate treatment strategy designed to raise your mood. Now there is some legitimacy with some of the issues raised with this approach, but its biggest failing is that it attempts to treat symptomology and in my opinion completely ignores the root cause determination of disease.

It's for that reason that I advocate that approaching this protocol unsupervised is dangerous, for it's eminently possible to exacerbate your mood symptoms and find yourself in a deeper black hole. I've accelerated my thought processes beyond imagination, I've lowered my mood significantly, I've made myself hyper and I've made myself sombulant using products prescribed via the mood cure, yet I have no idea if that was because of my underlying disease state or not.

What I do know is that whilst The Mood Cure is very informing, it falls short of a holistic treatment protocol the reason being: it focuses almost entirely upon brain function with some input about the adrenals, but ignores other possible origins of disease. That is it's failing as far as I'm concerned simply because it does not attempt to address holistically via scientific or clinical root cause analysis other disease states that can propagate shifts in our mood and/or lead to chronic depression expression at any point in our lives.

I have the power in me to be all that I was born to be and now I believe it !

Counselling

Having studied psychology for the best part of my adult life, there are not many counselling techniques that I've not studied, participated in or read about. The result of which is that I understand that it's very easy to either react and deny ownership of our emotions or drill down into them and analyse them to the far end of a fart. Safe to say that as a guy committed to my own development I underwent extensive personal counselling before my pre-diagnosed Lymes Disease which was driving me around the bend. Yet in all my dealings in this area I've only ever met two counsellors that I respected, because they were real people, they'd been through the mill themselves and yet they'd come through and out the other side.

The rest have been intellectual game playing cretins, complete bullshit merchants, hypocrites or charlatans of the highest order. So much so that I now advise anyone attending counselling to sit up and take note. If you're leaving a counselling session lower than you were before you went in, then the first thing you must do is cancel any further counselling session because it's not working or the counsellor hasn't got a clue. Either that or your organic diseased state is interfering with the process.

My view is as I've stated many times in this book, our thoughts are a product of our body's chemical process efficiencies. If something is affecting them, then our thoughts will not improve until we correct those processes. Anyone that's truly been through a major chronic emotional or depressive cycle will know that it's simply impossible to change your thoughts.

I am a mortal living amongst mortals and I too have rights and needs

That is the major stumbling block that I have with counselling. I disagree that the mind can cure or resolve a chronic diseased state, but once the chronic diseased state has been tackled, then the mind can certainly help with a holistic recovery. So if you're thinking about attending counselling as a means of trying to recover from chronic illness, I would say think again and only do so if you're 100% sure that the origin of your symptoms are emotional and not simply diseased state generated emotional symptomology. But you'll only know that for sure once you've tested and ruled out organic disease in the first place.

My view is *'Our mind is the victim of our toxic bodily load, it does not self generate toxic emotions or toxic thoughts, our mind is as happy and free as a bird at the point that we address all our body's toxic load'*.

I have the power in me to be all that I was born to be and now I believe it !

Hormone Replacement

When our bodies are under attack by illness or the sheer ferocity of life there is always the potential for our hormonal system to break down. When that happens we are presented with all sorts of physiological and emotional challenges which can be difficult at best and life sapping at worst. Facing that situation there is enough evidence to suggest that supplementation with small amounts of hormones and/or their precursors can be beneficial. Because of that I don't think there is a hormone or hormone precursor that I haven't taken in the past thirty years.

Now whilst I would never contest low dose supplementation of hormones and/or hormone precursors if an individual felt the need to do that, because I have received benefits from supplementing with low dose prednisolone, cortef and armour myself. I do through personal experience suggest that supplementing with pregnenolone, estrogens, (oestrogens) testosterone, DHEA and progesterone etc., should be avoided if at all possible. I say that simply because I've self supplemented with all the former hormones and to be honest it can be a very scary and unforgiving experience.

What's even more disturbing is that supplementing with low dose hormones and/or their precursors from my own personal experience actually exasperated my illness expressions. Therefore I would say to anyone interested in exploring supplementing with hormones and/or their precursors, take it very slowly, be sure of your research and above all; listen, monitor and record your physiological and emotional responses continuously. If you adhere to those simple guidelines you can ensure that at all times you're in total control.

I am a mortal living amongst mortals and I too have rights and needs

Thyriod / Adrenals

For me the endocrine system plays a significant part in chronic illness and I was lucky because I met some very decent private clinicians as I battled to stabilise my well being. Whilst there is absolutely no doubt that supervised support of the adrenals and thyroid can certainly help some conditions. There are significant issues globally with the treatment of endocrine issues such as hypothyroidism and hypoadrenalism and it is certainly possible to treat those conditions to good effect.

However, support of the endocrine system is not the great panacea that some people have been lured into believing. Inspirational success stories like Diane Holmes and her book *'Tears Behind Closed Doors'* have created buy in to these conditions to the detriment of conclusive clinical investigations. When I was exploring hypothyroidism it was simply desperate reading online, people trying to emulate Diane by medicating with Thyroxine or Armour yet unable to make any progress.

It was only as I began to bottom out my own illnesses that I realised why that was. You see, whilst the thyroid might be underperforming it should not be simply taken for granted that all associated symptoms are directly attributable to thyroid malfunction. The key for me is, support your thyroid and adrenals if you feel you need to, but if you're not improving then you need to test for possible originating diseases because it may well be that it's the diseases that are challenging your endocrine system and not your endocrine systems that is in a diseased state.

I have the power in me to be all that I was born to be and now I believe it !

Massage & Heller Work

As a committed amateur sportsman I always understood the significant part that sports and remedial massage played in my physical performance both as a footballer and runner. It has to be one of the best ways there is to help push the debris of exercise out of your tissues and into your lymphatic system. During my chronic illness however I spent thousands of pounds on remedial massage, desperately trying to get some degree of flexibility again back into my legs, arms, back, shoulders and neck. All to no avail, my muscles would begin to lock up again in most instances before I'd even left the treatment room.

It's absolutely insane the number of medical personnel who wrote me off with stress and the number of clinicians who did the exact same thing as Lymes Disease destroyed, through neurotoxicity induced inflammation, all flexibility in my body. That is the point I need to make, if massage is unable to relax your muscles, ignore any comments about your body being in a state of stress, you must test and continue to test for originators of disease e.g. Lymes Disease etc, until you find your answer.

Because there is absolutely no way that your body can fail to respond to massage if you're simply suffering from stress in the form of adrenal insufficiency.

I am a mortal living amongst mortals and I too have rights and needs

Samento

When I was diagnosed with Lymes Disease, samento was the first natural product that I was prescribed and it really did have a tremendous impact in terms of killing lymes. Samento's beneficial properties are mainly attributed to a group of actives called pentacyclic oxindole alkaloids (POA's) that act on the cellular immune system. In most Cat's Claw species, the presence of another group, the tetracyclic oxindole alkaloids (TOA's) greatly inhibits the action of the POA's yet Samento is certified to be 100% TOA free.

What does all that mean? Well it means that Samento is extremely potent, you only need to take small amounts of it to ensure that its antimicrobial effects kick in. Whilst that may sound great in the treatment of lymes, it is but equally its not. You see, the problem with Lymes Disease is that it disrupts lots of systems in the body ultimately disabling the bodies detoxing capabilities. This means that whilst you kill the Lymes Disease when taking samento, the probability is that your condition will not be significantly improved because the byproduct of that treatment regime is a tenfold increase in your mobile/circulating neuro-toxin load.

In conclusion whilst Samento has a part to play if you choose to use it in your recovery from lymes. Simply supplementing with it will not bring about any form of recovery unless your detox capabilities are first enhanced and supported through your entire treatment protocol for life.

I have the power in me to be all that I was born to be and now I believe it !

Antibiotics

When herbal treatments didn't bring about the sort of recovery I needed from my Lymes Disease I explored orthodox medications such as antibiotics. Despite what you may read or be told that Lymes Disease can be cured with a short course of doxycycline, amoxicillin or minocycline, I'm clinically advising you now as a chronic lymes sufferer such statements are misleading and absurdly wrong wrong wrong. What they are capable of doing within days is to create a wide range of side effects including ototoxicity of the inner ear. That may mean nothing to you, but it should because it is irreversible damage to your inner ear and could result in you having to cope with rotary vertigo for the rest of your life as well as trying to cope with lymes.

My view is for chronic conditions such as Lymes Disease, stay as far away from antibiotics as you possibly can. There may be a place for them in other situations, but for chronic situations they're a complete waste of space.

Reiki & Spiritual Healing

Reiki is the name given to a system of natural healing which evolved in Japan from the experience and dedication of Dr Mikao Usui. He spent most of his life practicing and teaching Reiki. It is believed by many Reiki practitioners that it's possible to heal at any level of being, be that, physical, mental, emotional or spiritual.

Unfortunately, despite being a Reiki practitioner myself, it didn't help me, despite visiting more than a few practitioners in my pursuit of relief. Neither did spiritual healing; a situation which challenged me to my core since I had witnessed and believed in the spiritual dimension all my life. I was shocked that at my time of greatest need instead of the light forces coming in to help me it was only the dark forces that saw fit to attach themselves to me.

Now we can't be anything other than what we were born to be and I've been either cursed or blessed by the vast range and depths of powers and skills that I've experienced. All that I say on the matter of Reiki is stay open and if works for you then accept it, because if it works then as far as you should be concerned that's really okay in the greater scheme of things.

I have the power in me to be all that I was born to be and now I believe it !

Marshall Protocol

I tried this protocol when I was making no progress at all with my lymes treatment. The premise of the protocol is to block all inflammation process whilst killing all cellular microorganisms and bacteria's. The two hormones cited as drivers of the inflammatory process are Angiotensin II and the seco-steroid 1,25-dihydroxyvitamin-D. Blocking Angiotensin II apparently weakens immune evading bacteria to the point where they can be more easily killed, and reducing the 1,25-D makes it harder for the bacteria to slip in and out of the cells that they have infected. The angiotensin receptor blocker Olmesartan dosed approximately every six hours is used to block the Angiotensin II receptors in the inflamed tissue and small doses of Minocycline can then be ingested to finish the bacteria off. So does this treatment work? Well it certainly lowers inflammation but as far as improving health, well I'm not sure.

I didn't like the side effects of this protocol, I got to the point where I could hardly walk because of the lowering in blood pressure caused by the Olmesartan and I got very cheesed off with the vertigo cause by Minocycline.

Within a few weeks I didn't value the Marshall Protocol at all and I certainly didn't like the Marshall Protocol online culture. I would never recommend this treatment option to anyone but if people wish to explore it I would simply say to them; by all means go for it, but be careful whatever you do.

I am a mortal living amongst mortals and I too have rights and needs

Mickel Therapy

I explored this treatment because there was a lot of hype around it at the time I was looking for answers. The main premise of the Mickel Therapy is Hypothalamitis. The therapy postulates that when 'infected' the hypothalamus thinks the body is under attack, so it will tell the body to produce chemicals to prepare muscles for fight or flight. That's a very long winded way of saying that your endocrine system is on full alert. The therapy revolves around you listening to your body and then telling it to calm down and in doing so your body starts to heal.

Well sorry not for me I'm afraid; there's no way on this green planet that anyone suffering from a chronic degenerative illness is going to recover from this therapy. But that's not to say that it doesn't have some validity, because there appears to be enough evidence to suggest that the therapy does work for individuals suffering from mild neurosis.

So if it works for them than I say great, but I would never recommend the therapy despite Dr David Mickel coming across on the surface to me as a thoroughly decent guy.

I have the power in me to be all that I was born to be and now I believe it !

Homeopathy

With absolutely no faith in the medical industry I explored homeopathy because passed experiences had sort of indicated that it had some validity. Unfortunately I had prediagnosed Lymes Disease symptoms when I committed myself fully to this treatment approach and it simply failed my wholesale. My body was in a hypometabolic state which meant I reacted dreadfully to everything thing I ingested including all things homeopathic.

The result of which I have to say pushed me further into a diseased state as my adrenals etc., simply couldn't cope with the increased emotional load from its so called clearing fall out. I had many bad experiences with homeopaths and because of that I feel very strongly about some of their attitudes etc.

So if anyone from the homeopathic world ever says to you that the remedy is not responsible for the reaction your experiencing it's your body. Look them straight in the eye and ask them this, 'Did you or did you not give me a remedy' and they will naturally reply 'Yes' Your answer must then be, 'Well I took your remedy and that's why I feel like this, now can we please stop all the clap trap and bullshit, because I need some help'.

The reason that I've mentioned that is because there are some very talented homeopaths out there, but equally there are a lot of quacks and I even lived with and allowed myself to be treated by a quack during the most dreadful period of and in my life. The quacks are both a danger to themselves and a danger to society and trust me on this I saw one or two full on quacks.

I am a mortal living amongst mortals and I too have rights and needs

Anyway enough of that, so where do I sit in terms of homeopathic treatment? Well, my view is it can't clear or help anyone with a chronic bacterial, viral, fungal or neurotoxin load. But as the condition becomes more under control, then that's the point homeopathy comes into its own, supporting the patient though there coming to terms and letting go process and in my opinion nothing more.

I believe in the power of homeopathy when used in the right situation and prescribed by a first class homeopath. But when used in the wrong situation or prescribed by 'homeo-quacks' it's very, very dangerous and a complete waste of money and time.

I have the power in me to be all that I was born to be and now I believe it !

CranioSacral

This therapy is a gentle, hands-on method of evaluating and enhancing the function of a physiological body system called the CranioSacral system. The CranioSacral system is comprised of the membranes and cerebrospinal fluid which form the fluid-filled sac around the core of the nervous system, surrounding, nourishing, and protecting the brain and spinal cord. Using a touch generally no heavier than the weight of a small coin, skilled practitioners can monitor this rhythm at key body areas to pinpoint the source of an obstruction or stress.

The problem with this treatment approach is that it's absolutely of no use when the body is in a diseased state such as with Lymes Disease. This is because the Lymes and its neurotoxin load just keep placing an exceptional amount of stress upon the body. Frequently I found that some CranioSacral practitioners were not able to accept that it was a disease and not me the patient who was preventing progress using this approach.

Moreover there's a practitioner whom I visited many times in the Lake District prior to my Lymes Disease diagnosis that I will gladly rip limb from limb if I ever meet him again for all the ignorant abuse he offloaded onto me. I can't believe that I paid some anal quack a lot of money, to weekly verbally abuse me about my personal psychology, citing that and it as the reason I was in such a desperate state.

I am a mortal living amongst mortals and I too have rights and needs

Rife Technology

Desperate to get ontop of my Lymes Disease I purchased a Rife Machine from South Africa at a cost of £1800 pounds plus import duty of £250 pounds or so. The Rife machine was developed by Dr. Royal R. Rife in the 1930s and used a variable frequency, pulsed radio transmitter to produce mechanical resonance within the cells of the physical body. The Rife machine was, in its time, a pioneering front-runner for what today is the basis of energetic medicine. Rife discovered he could use specific electro-magnetic frequencies to kill a bacteria or viruses without causing damage to the surrounding tissue.

The portable rife machines of today also work on the principle of sympathetic resonance, which states that if there are two similar objects and one of them is vibrating, the other will begin to vibrate as well, even if they are not touching. In the same way that a sound wave can induce resonance in a crystal glass and ultra-sound can be used to destroy gall-stones.

Rife machines use sympathetic resonance to physically vibrate the cells of the parasite resulting in possible elimination. Now the reason I went for a rife machine over a Dr. Hulda Clark Zapper was because nothing I'd read or heard convinced me that that the Zapper was able to create anywhere near the breadths and depths of frequencies that the modern rife machines could.

So did and does the Rife machine work? Oh yes without any shadow of a doubt, the only problem is that it kills so much lymes and interrelated organisms that the herx reactions are extremely intense. When I first started using my Rife machine I was a very ill guy yet the results of using my Rife machine simply knocked me on my back as my body was swamped with neuro and bio toxins.

I have the power in me to be all that I was born to be and now I believe it !

It wasn't until I'd re-energized my detox capabilities that I was able to use my Rife machine with any degree of comfort.

The really good thing about the Rife machine when using it to treat Lymes is that the Lymes cannot change its form when under attack like it does with herbs and other treatment. Because the Rife Machine simply vibrates it to death whatever forms the damn disease chooses to adopt.

Would I recommend use of a Rife machine? Well yes I would but I think I would suggest that people buy one between them and take turns rather than forking out over 2k. It's a lot of money and whilst you'll have it for years, it does a lot of sitting around when not in use and I don't think that makes for a good investment because of the initial financial expense.

I am a mortal living amongst mortals and I too have rights and needs

Detoxing & Blood Cleaning

There was a point in my health decline and numerous unsuccessful recovery treatment protocols that I tried many detox approaches and many blood cleaning approaches. So much so that when I look back now it's simply staggering because I never made any form of improvement for all the expense and suffering I endured. I now understand that attempting to detox via the various methods we read or see online, on TV or in magazines is simply not the right approach for chronically ill people.

You see, when we become infected with lymes or diseases of that nature, our livers and/or our overall detox capabilities are significantly damaged or compromised. That means that we move into a toxic body state because we're constantly being poisoned by the disease generated toxins that are constantly being circulating or laid down in the fat rich tissues of our body. Unfortunately the vast majority of so called detox experts don't fully understand how our body processes work beyond, the liver, gallbladder or pancreas if you're lucky.

They simply don't understand mitochondria blockage or the breakdown in methylation and sulfanation processes. They don't understand liver anger or herxing with any degree of acuity. All of them in general make ridiculous claims that after one week or one month detoxing on their regime you'll feel remarkably much better. When in fact you won't if you've got a chronic toxic body but there is a significant chance that you'll feel much worse.

I have the power in me to be all that I was born to be and now I believe it !

My view is simply this; explore anything and everything you wish to explore in terms of detoxing, but do not under any circumstance undergo any form of rigorous detox regime if your suffering from a chronic illness. Because the price you'll pay is far greater than you could ever know i.e. significantly increased symptomology, increase fat gain around the middle despite claims to the contrary, greater fatigue, anger, depression and no improvement at all.

I am a mortal living amongst mortals and I too have rights and needs

Shoemaker Neurotoxin Cleanse

This treatment protocol developed by Dr. Richie Shoemaker is based around the real phenomenon of biotoxins causing continuation of illness in the majority of chronically illness patients. The protocol advocates taking the medication Questran (cholestyramine) which is powder that acts like a sponge binding circulating toxins within the body to it. Questran is often prescribed to pull cholesterol out of people's bodies and is easy to ingest.

Now I tried this protocol because I believe in Toxic Body Syndrome *TBS* but unfortunately for me it didn't work at the time although I was only given a very short prescription of Questran from my GP. Nevertheless if anyone felt that they were experiencing TBS, I would certainly suggest that they read up on the Shoemaker protocol because there is great validity in lowering toxin loads in the chronically ill.

I have the power in me to be all that I was born to be and now I believe it !

Sauna Therapy

In an aid to help with detoxing I underwent years of wet sauna therapy and to be honest it did absolutely nothing for me. When I switched to a Far Infra Red sauna however the results were far more dramatic, so much so that I bought one and use one to this day. The infra red sauna is cheap to run, requires only a standard electrical plug point, its easy to sit in, stimulates a significant increase in sweat and toxin mobilization and I cannot recommend it highly enough.

Like all other conjunctive therapies though it needs to be treated with respect. When using a FIR we need to support our bodies with colloidal minerals and vitamins etc., we need to hydrate and we need to make sure that the sauna is kept clean and that we shower immediately upon leaving the sauna to ensure that we minimize re-assimilation of toxins.

In summation the difference between wet and FIR saunas is that the wet penetrates the skins surface and offers very little detox support. Whereas the FIR penetrates deep into the body and mobilizes and pushes both fat and water soluble toxins out of your body and in essence reduces your overall toxic load.

Methylation

One of the areas of research that really stimulated my interest as I desperately tried to get on top of my neurotoxin load was the issue of our methylation process. Our methylation process is the primary driving force behind so many processes in our body's attempt to detox harmful substances. Effective 'markers' for methylation are:

(a) Whole blood histamine ref. levels 40-70 mcg/dL.

And

(b) Absolute Basophils ref. levels 30-50.

In terms of determining how effective our methylation processes, are elevated histamine and/or elevated basophils by default indicate undermethylation and that's not really good news. Methylation is involved in DNA synthesis, masking and unmasking of DNA detoxification, heavy mental detoxification, nerve myelination, carnitine and coenzyme Q 10 synthesis. Therefore it's essential if we are to have good health that we have an effective methylation process. But what can we do if our methylation processes are not working? Well current thinking is that we can kick start our methylation processes with the supplementation of precursors of the methylation process including:

- Folic Acid and Vitamin B12.

- Trimethylglycine (natural sugar beet source).

- Vitamin B6 (combination of Pyridoxine HCL and Pyridoxal 5 phosphate).

I have the power in me to be all that I was born to be and now I believe it !

- Choline (combination of Choline bitartrate and phosphatidyl choline).

- Taurine.

- Magnesium (Magnesium Glycinate).

- Zinc (Zinc Monomethionate).

- Copper (Copper Glycinate).

Now it would be fair to assume that by supporting our methylation process with those supplements that everything would sort of resolve itself and our methylation would recover. Well that would be the case if it was as simple as that but its not and it's not because some of us have dysfunctional methylation processes from birth. So much so that if we start pushing the methylation process over and above our bodily needs we can easily push ourselves into a much more dangerous state. As I've discussed earlier undermethylation can result in high histamine which can present as:

- Obsessive-compulsive tendencies.

- Oppositional-defiant disorder.

- Seasonal depression.

All of which are associated with low serotonin levels. If we push our methylation process to much though in an attempt to improve our detoxing capabilities we can drastically reduce our histamine levels. So what you may ask that's surely a good result isn't it?

I am a mortal living amongst mortals and I too have rights and needs

Well in truth its most definitely not. You see, very quickly you could end up with suicidal depression amongst other things, because healthy levels of histamine are vital for so many functions in our bodies. That's why playing around un-supervised with our methylation process is unwise at best and extremely dangerous at worst; because with in a matter of days you may easily find that your thought processes are like those from another planet. In essence it's important to understand when pushing our methylation process the difference between histadelia and histadelics. So let me wrap up the biochemistry of high and low histamine so that you have a much clearer understanding of the point I'm trying to make, you see:

- Histadelia is a condition which is characterized by elevated serum levels of histamine and basophils processes similar symptoms to those covered early in pyroluria.

Whereas:

- Histadelics are people with low histamine and typical symptoms include under-achievement, more severe thought disorder and hallucinations, paranoid thoughts with less pronounced obsessions, suicidal depression, cyclic or suicidal depression, and anxiety.

Clearly therefore; when attempting to manipulate your methylation process, you must take that initiative onboard with great caution, because the dynamics of histamine balancing are extremely complex.

I have the power in me to be all that I was born to be and now I believe it !

Now look, I've briefly covered a number of treatment options in this chapter but to be honest, I would say to anyone thinking of undergoing any form of treatment option. Before you commence your treatment option or protocol you must make sure that:

- You understand the science behind what you're doing.

- You are sure that it's the right approach for you.

- You have appropriate clinical support.

- You're going to be able to make the decisions you may need to make if at any point complications set in for you.

Above all things take NO notice of anecdotal evidence or retorts, including any passions expressed in this book. Because you must personally prove, validate and ratify everything you're about to undertake in your treatment approach, because your wellbeing and even your life depends upon it.

The bottom line at the end of the day is that your wellbeing and future happiness rests solely and at all times with you. So be honest and true to yourself and make sure that whatever route or options you take you remain always focused and in control.

But more than just that, I wish for you the best of luck and hopefully the return to that level of health and wellbeing that we all so richly deserve.

I am a mortal living amongst mortals and I too have rights and needs

The key is to remember that the process of healing can be accelerated when we take control of effective root cause analysis etc, a dynamic clearly profiled in my pictorial healing times lines (a) and (b) and qualifying in (c) and (d) the dynamic of understanding whether you're on the correct treatment rationale for you or not.

You see; there are no great rewards for anyone in unnecessary suffering because it adds very little to our life at all. Therefore we must always listen to our body and our higher self and learn to understand the truth and/or substance of everything we hear, read, see or feel in our body as we pursue our quest of a greater and better quality of life. Without that personal commitment, there is no real potential for whole body healing, because the process of healing both begins and ends with our ability to self nurture, self solve and self support our bodies throughout our entire and overall healing process. Because in truth, we're the only ones who can give it our full and highly considered attention and that's because, invariably we're the only ones who truly care anyway.

I have the power in me to be all that I was born to be and now I believe it !

My Actual Healing Time Line
Time Line (a)

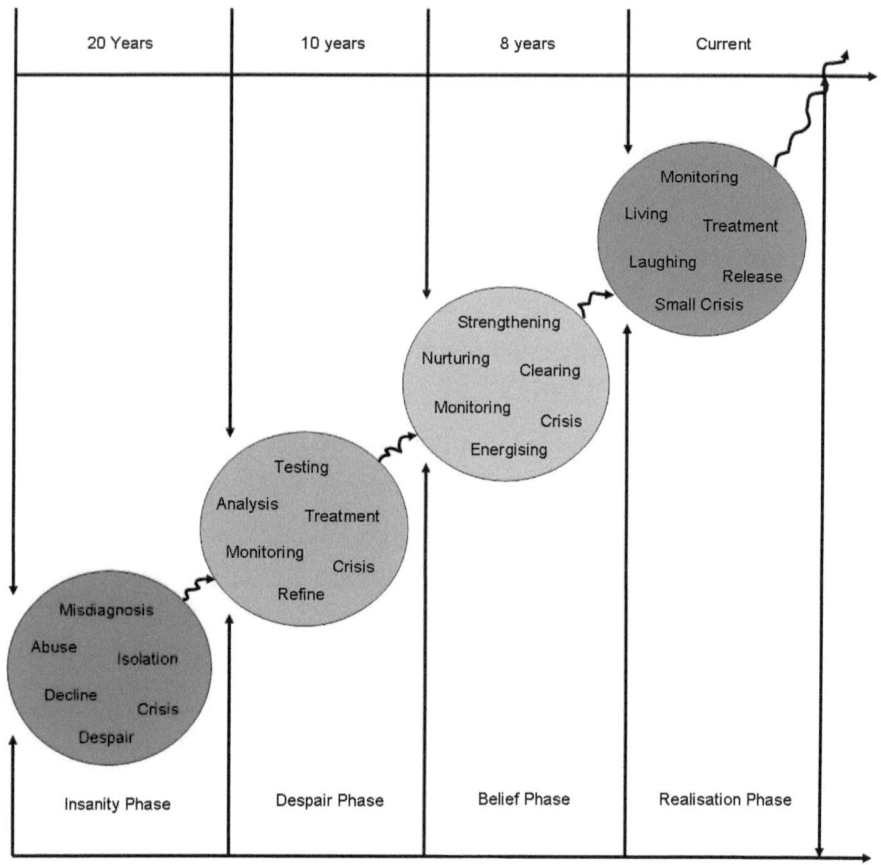

Time is only the great healer when our healing time is spent well

I am a mortal living amongst mortals and I too have rights and needs

Possible Healing Time Line
Time Line (b)

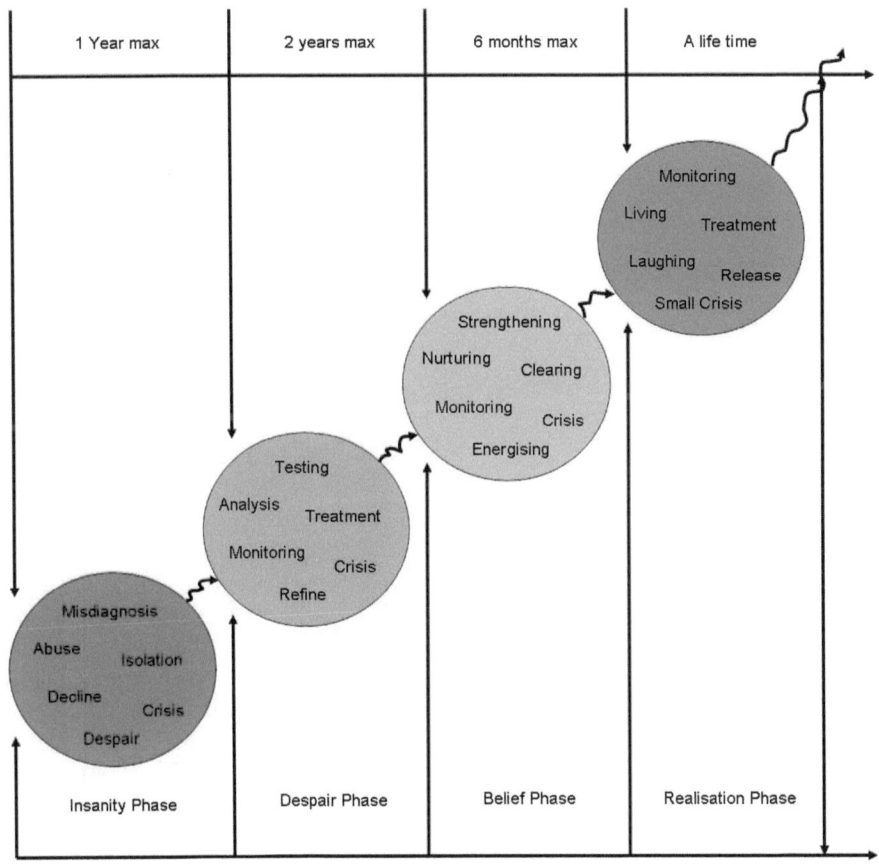

Time is only the great healer when our healing time is spent well

I have the power in me to be all that I was born to be and now I believe it !

Inappropriate Treatment Time Line 4U
Time Line (c)

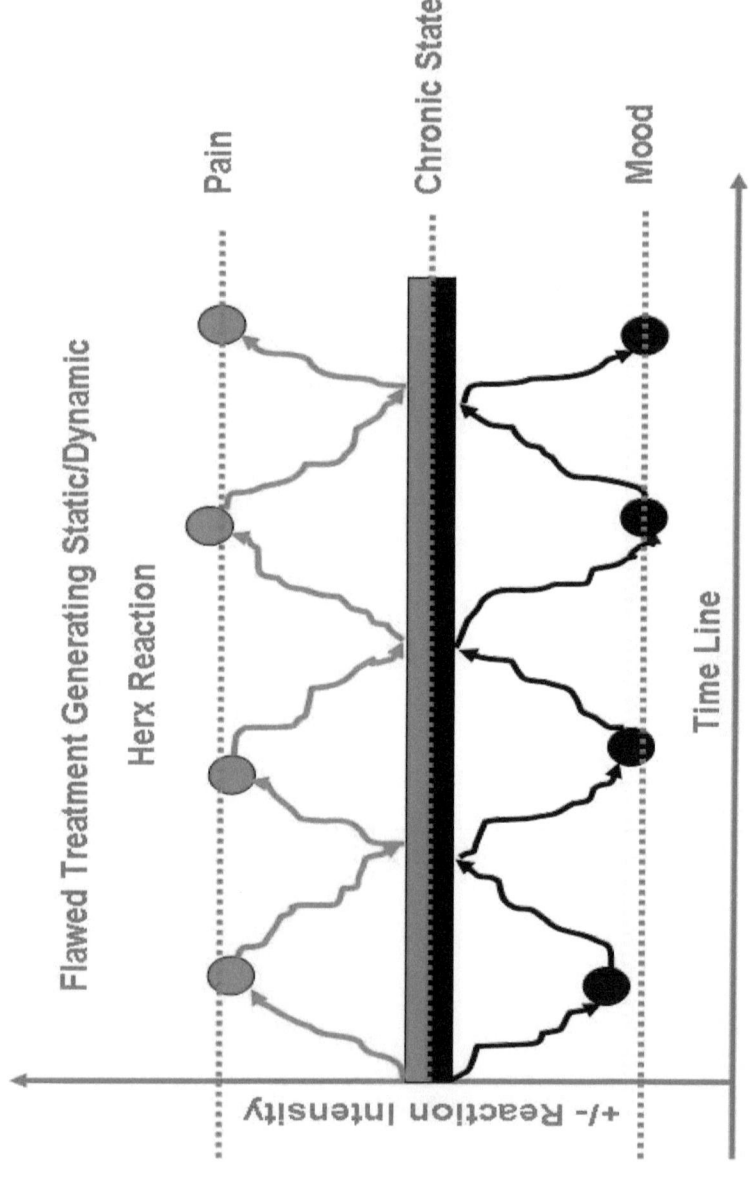

I am a mortal living amongst mortals and I too have rights and needs

Correct Treatment Time Line 4U
Time Line (d)

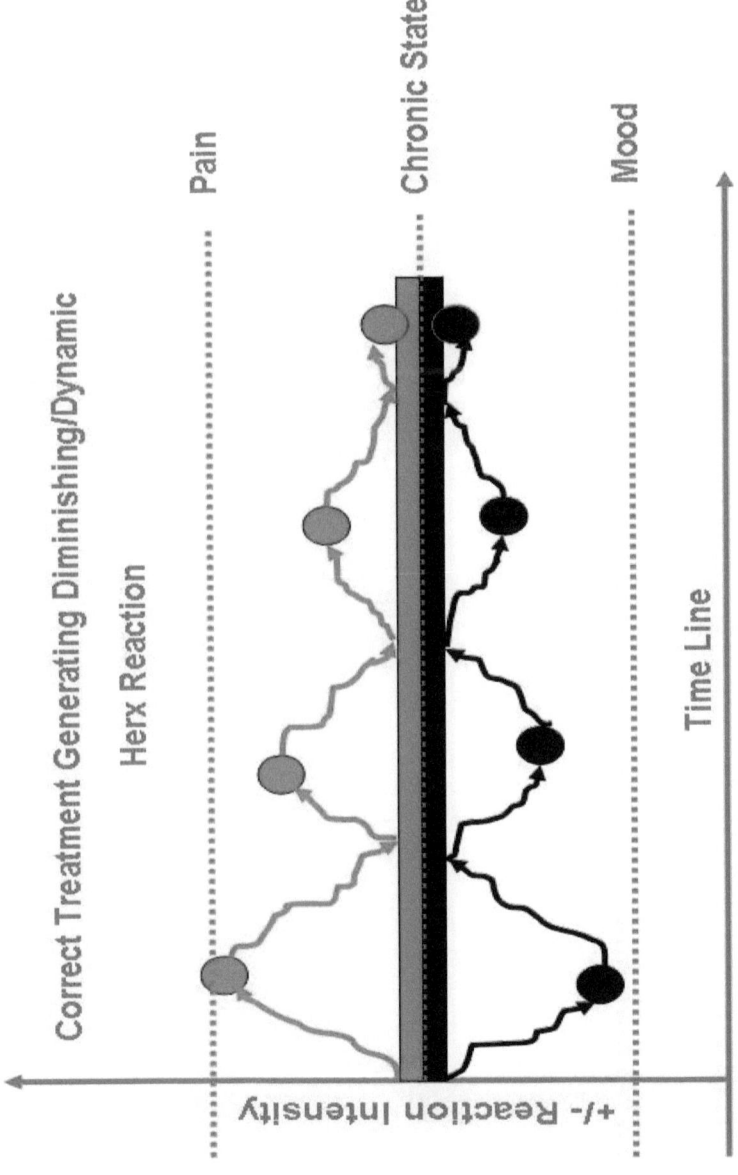

I have the power in me to be all that I was born to be and now I believe it !

I am a mortal living amongst mortals and I too have rights and needs

(9) ANALYTICAL TESTING

I've made great play throughout this book of the need for effective testing and re-testing if necessary, to enable effective diagnosis of underlying diseased states. Yet whilst those tests can take many forms including: imaging and bodywork. I believe that the key to identifying the root cause of any chronic condition begins with effective blood and biochemical marker analysis. The clinic that I used for my detailed blood analysis via my private GP Dr. Sarah Myhill referrals was 'Biolab Medical Unit UK'.

Biolab Medical Unit is a; medical referral laboratory specializing in nutritional and environmental medicine which is located in the heart of the West End of London. They are a nutritional biochemistry laboratory measuring vitamin and mineral levels, toxic metals, other biochemical levels that are related to the availability of vitamins, minerals and other nutrients. They have an extensive range of profiles for assessing the effects of twenty-first century lifestyles on our bodies and are dedicated to assisting doctor's sort out their patients' problems in a way that does not rely on drugs as a first line of treatment. Biolab apply modern scientific laboratory analytical methods to establish what imbalances there are in the bodies of those who are suffering ill-health or non-optimum health, so that these imbalances may be addressed via nutritional and non-drug means, with the aim of achieving good health or, at least, improving the quality of life and minimizing suffering.

I have the power in me to be all that I was born to be and now I believe it !

I would therefore suggest that it's worth visiting their website at www.biolab.co.uk/ for a more detailed overview of their services, staff and publications etc. However please note that Biolab Medical Unit (UK) is a referral unit and will only perform tests requested by practitioners registered with;

- The General Medical Council.

- The General Dental Council.

- The General Osteopathic Council.

- The General Chiropractic Council.

All test reports will be sent to your practitioner as Biolab will not enter into direct discussions with you about your results, although they are happy to discuss their findings in relation to your tests with your practitioner. It's important to note that I have absolutely no commercial, professional or personal arrangement with Biolab Medical Unit or any other analytical service provider. Furthermore those services providers will be completely unaware of my personal use of their services or my recommendation of their services. I would nevertheless strongly urge any individual suffering from a chronic health condition and wishing to undergo private blood investigations etc., to discuss their case with their medical/clinical service provider and request that they enter into discussions with respective analytical service providers such as Biolab. But be under no illusion that you may find that an uphill battle because medics in general traditionally poo poo anything that deviates from their own ignorant perspectives. If that is the outcome of your discussions then you have only three choices open to you:

I am a mortal living amongst mortals and I too have rights and needs

(a) Stay with your current service provider.

(b) Secure more appropriate service support.

Or

(c) Give up completely on life.

Ultimately as the masters of our own health and happiness we must make the choices we feel are best for us and in that we must be prepared to stand or fall, live or die by the choices we choose to make.

I have the power in me to be all that I was born to be and now I believe it !

I am a mortal living amongst mortals and I too have rights and needs

(10) A CASE FOR SELF EXPLORATION

Now then; there's been a lot of words, a lot of postulations and lot of my prejudicial views in this book thus far. But I'm not naive enough to think that anyone reading this book will fully understand and feel completely at ease with the points that I've been making about my alternative approach to chronic illness expression eradication. Nevertheless if some of what I've had to say has stimulated your thought processes about your current and/or past chronic illness expressions, then I've managed at least to realise one of my main initial objectives. You see; I believe that when we begin to explore well trodden boundaries within our lives and psyche that we've previously considered as rigid constraints. We're frequently rewarded either directly or indirectly with completely different and rewarding insights about things that we've either taken for granted and/or written off has having no overall validity.

I have the power in me to be all that I was born to be and now I believe it !

That being said I'm now going to cover in the final few pages of this book a simple approach to chronic illness detection that may challenge your perceptions of your current or past chronic illness expressions to their core. The key as ever to my postulations of securing better health is personal ownership and sensibility to your overall wellbeing and under no circumstance putting yourself at any significant risk. You see; no one should have to live with irresolvable chronic illness expression, because it is neither a karmic lesson nor an opportunity to grow, but that doesn't mean to say we should take risks in our attempts to recover for the same because in doing so there is always the potential of making our situation much much worse.

I am a mortal living amongst mortals and I too have rights and needs

Poor quality of life and health are nothing more than blights upon our lives and so no matter which way anyone chooses to look at it. The expression of unresolved chronic illness expression in society at large needs to be removed from our society and psyche completely right now. Not tomorrow, not next week or next month or next year, but today, this minute, right now. Because despite what anyone ever says to you about the seemingly irresolvable nature of your illness, you can get better if you draw upon all the skills and intellect at your disposal and commit to an holistic program of physical well being though disease originator eradication.

We all deserve good health and what's more we have a right to it and that's not open to question, but the word on the street and the word that I'm proclaiming loud and clear is; 'CAUTION' at all times, because without that there is always the real possibility of antagonizing your already fragile well being capabilities. If we wish to recover from chronic ill health we must take our health seriously and under no circumstance undertake any investigation or treatment activity without suitable supervision and/or medical/clinical guidance. When we commit to an educated and scientific regime of testing, investigation, qualification and treatment, we're actually providing our body and our resolve with all that they need to bring about a state of physical wellbeing, Amen.

I have the power in me to be all that I was born to be and now I believe it !

In pursuit of recovery from my chronic illnesses I was forced to look at illness from a completely different perspective to that which I was brain washed with as a child. Subsequently, my personal health struggles have proven to me:

(a) Just how insidiously corrupt that brain washing was.

And

(b) Just how appallingly ignorant our medics really are.

The simple fact of the matter is that:

(a) Few medics truly understand the dynamics of illness.

And

(b) Few are prepared to shift their perception of illness preferring instead to adhere to the medical clap trap they bought into as part of their so called medical training.

Because of that it's very difficult when we're chronically ill to get any form of logical or scientific input from the medical industry full stop. Patients are written off at best and blamed at worst when presenting themselves to a medic with anything more than a cold, stomach bug or pain in the chest. It's like medics simply don't get illness at all, it's like illness is a great mystery to them which I struggle to comprehend really.

They don't seem to understand cause and effect, they don't seem to understand variable input dynamics and they don't understand basic physiology over and above basic anatomical understanding. In essence I've simply never come across an industry with such high levels of occupational ignorance towards the service it provides and for me that truly marks that industry as antediluvian *(old fashioned)* and as such no longer worthy of my respect.

Therefore when we are faced with chronic illness it's imperative that we take full ownership of our problem because it is the only sure fire way of making any progress. You see, chronic illness has many generators and we must understand that dynamic if we are to ever fully recover. Happily the majority of what we need to know as laymen in terms of illness is not rocket science either; it's just common sense, body monitoring and holistic treatment management.

So; you've read my highly opinionated postulations in terms of the originators and drivers of chronic illness expression, the question now is are you up for testing your historical perceptions. If so let's explore that receptivity in this chapter.

I have the power in me to be all that I was born to be and now I believe it !

Do you know there is one sure fire thing about anyone suffering from chronic illness expression and that is; sufferers will do and take anything they can to remove it from their life. The majority in the end resort to a whole raft of escapist options because living in their body is simply beyond mortal endurance at times. It's not untypical for a sufferer to indulge and self indulge in a wide range of escapist pursuits some of which include:

- Exercise.
- Deviant acts.
- Drugs.
- Cigarettes.
- Alcohol.
- Orthodox medication.
- Herbal supplements.
- Homeopathy.

And even

- Suicide attempts.

Whilst others commit to

- Suicide completions.

I am a mortal living amongst mortals and I too have rights and needs

Such is the suffering of those, experiencing unrelenting, chronic ill health that for most their only constant thought is that of finding somehow or some way of detaching themselves from its grasp. As a former chronic illness sufferer, I know only too well the depth of despair that chronic illness can push you into when there is not a treatment, a medication, a supplement, an activity or self destruct approach that does not remove your major presenting symptoms. I truly know what it's like to live in a body when NOTHING and I mean NOTHING even remotely diminishes the impact of chronic illness upon your entire being. Nevertheless I'm stating firmly for the record that it's possible to lower chronic illness expression rapidly. In fact it's possible to feel better than you've ever felt in your life before, because at the point you address the underlying cause of your illness your recovery profile picks hitherto unthinkable momentum. Yet the approach that I prescribe is unlike any of the majority of orthodox options you may have encounter before because it does not include:

- Self beasting through Psychoanalysis.

Or

- Detachment though 'Somnolence' inducing concoctions.

Or even

- A combination of both ridiculous approaches.

I have the power in me to be all that I was born to be and now I believe it !

You see, my Raphael's Treatment Protocol RTP is based upon looking at chronic illness expression objectively and doing your utmost to uncover via root cause analysis the physical generator and/or generators of chronic illness expression before even looking at treating the symptoms of that disease generated diseased state. That is not to say that the sufferer is left in purgatory as is the case with current treatment approaches. Because the diminishment of negative symptom expression within hours is the short term goal of RTP, and that I may add is not some grandiose statement without substance because in reality it will be proven as fact. You see; if your original and/or presenting symptoms are the derivative of disease expression, which there is a great possibility that they are; then very simple, very effective and very safe bodily testing will prove that to you.

Thereafter RTP focuses upon the sustainability of underlying disease eradication whilst supporting the body through effective and re-energized removal of all associated toxic loads from the body. Note however that there are no ridiculous detox regimes in the RTP, no regimes of excessive supplement ingestion, but there is a need for whole body analysis and with that the chronic illness sufferer must accept there is an initial cost.

Extract Summary from the Raphael Treatment Protocol

1. You must have access to and be supervised by a suitably qualified practitioner.

2. You must NOT stop any treatment protocol you're currently undertaking until your analysis results have been compiled.

3. You must be prepared to accept that you will have to pay for several highly specialised blood and bodily function tests including:

    i. Mitochondria Analysis.
    ii. Viral Analysis.
    iii. Chlamydia Analysis.
    iv. Lymes Disease Analysis.
    v. Syphilis Analysis.
    vi. Fungal Analysis.
    vii. Methylation Analysis.
    viii. Sulphanation Analysis.
    ix. Thyroid Analysis.

    And

    x. A 24 hour Saliva Adrenal Function test.

4. You must be prepared to look objectively at your results with your practitioner and understand exactly what's happening and/or going on in your body.

I have the power in me to be all that I was born to be and now I believe it !

5. You must be prepared to undertake supervised treatment regimes designed to:

    i. Quash any microorganism disease states.
    ii. Support and energize any diseased organ states.
    iii. Support your bodies detoxing capabilities.

6. Monitor your body at every stage of your treatment protocol because as covered in the TBS chapter it's important to know where you're at.

7. Above all be gentle with yourself because the road to recovery is full of ups and downs during the process of disease eradication, toxin removal and whole body system re-energization.

Be under no illusion that at the point you begin to address any underlying disease states and commence the process of bio/lipo toxin removal from your body you will begin to feel much better almost immediately. Thereafter windows of freedom from chronic illness expression will become more frequent until chronic illness expression is nothing more than far a distant episode from your past. Now look I'm not naive to think that anyone reading this chapter will fully understand the point I'm making about my alternative approach to chronic illness eradication. But there is a very simple test that anyone suffering from chronic illness can do if they wish to explore a new way of understanding their condition and I qualify that for you on the next page.

I am a mortal living amongst mortals and I too have rights and needs

Take a small quantity of the suggested products re: below over let's say one to four days. The products I'm referring to are natural yet highly potent and they can be bought online or from any good health food store. All the products I'm about to suggest are antimicrobial, antibacterial and anti-inflammatory which means that they will immediately kill foreign invaders whilst reducing initially some of any directly or indirectly associated inflammation. They are:

- One tea spoon of Higher Nature 'MSM organic Sulphur Crystals' in water morning and night.

Or

- 2-5 drops NutraMedix 'Samento' in water morning and night.

Or

- 2-5 drops NutraMedix 'Cumanda' in water morning and night.

Or

- 2-5 drops Higher Nature 'Citricidal' Grapefruit Seed Liquid Extract in water morning and night.

It should be noted that I have absolutely no commercial or clinical/medical arrangement with either Higher Nature or NutraMedix including any other directly or indirectly associated party. I'm merely citing their products simply because I found them to work well for me.

I have the power in me to be all that I was born to be and now I believe it !

If you have an underlying disease which is responsible and/or contributing to your chronic illness expression then the result of taking small doses of the suggested products should be;

1. An immediate lifting in mood and may even move your mood slightly into a hyper or manic mode.

And

2. A reduction in bodily tension and pain and in some instance tension and pain may simply disappear.

However

3. The sufferer's mood will be drastically lowered again within a 8 / 12 hour window and all associated pain will increase with additional pain being generated in new and strange locations.

Now the reason all that happens time after time is because that is the standard Herxheimer Reaction (HR) that people with chronic disease states incur at the point they begin to address their diseased state. It's a toxic reaction generated in the body by toxins being released from dead or decaying parasites, fungus, viruses, bacteria or other pathogens. As these toxins circulate in our body, it is not uncommon to experience flu-like symptoms including headache, joint and muscle pain, body aches, sore throat, general malaise, sweating, chills, nausea or other symptoms. This is normal and indicates that parasites, fungus, viruses, bacteria or other pathogens are being effectively killed off.

I am a mortal living amongst mortals and I too have rights and needs

The biggest battle we all face in recovering from disease expression via RTP is dealing with the HR in a way that enables us to function and ensure that we can continue to medicate and support our bodies through what is a truly hellish situation. I myself have arrived at that point now because after years of self treating and suffering I've found the formula that allows me to kill my bodily invaders whilst supporting my defective detox capabilities via a number of gentle treatment protocols not least of which includes the use of a far infrared sauna daily. But you can read more about that in my book *Raphael's Treatment Protocol.*

I have the power in me to be all that I was born to be and now I believe it !

Now there is one further important point I need to make here in relation to the support of chronic illness suffers who are clearly experiencing some degree of endocrine system insufficiency and that is I completely agree with the medication of small doses of hormones in terms of:

1. Hydrocortisol and/or prednisolone to support the adrenals, *which can be purchased online without a prescription.*

And

2. Synthetic Armour to support the thyroid, *which can be purchased online without a prescription.*

So whilst pompous medics will cry foul on that matter and cite my support of such medications as evidence of my cavalier and ludicrous approach to wellness. All I can say is that in controlled and supervised dosage both medication offer far greater whole body health benefits than many well known prescription medications that are given out willy nilly. In fact they are probably less dangerous when handled with integrity than:

- Alcohol.

- Cigarettes.

- High fat foods.

And

I am a mortal living amongst mortals and I too have rights and needs

- Controlled substances such as:

    I. Crack cocaine.

    II. Heroine.

    III. Marijuana etc.

All off which can be purchased with ease and consumed in completely irresponsibly fashions, all imposing greater harm onto already impoverished capabilities of sufferers with any form of chronic illness. All appear to be addictive and whilst some have a more direct impact upon specific organs, i.e. lungs, brain and liver. Unfortunately cocaine, heroine and marijuana carry a much deadlier addictive tendency and can even damage many areas in the brain not least of which includes Gaba receptors and associated neuro-networks leading to emotional/psychological complications.

Now look I've sort of laboured that point for one very specific reason, and that is if your tests prove you're suffering from adrenal insufficiency there is absolutely no way that a medic will provide you with small dose endocrine system support and so at that point your way forward is entirely up to you. Personally however I say stay well clear of the cigarettes, alcohol, high fat foods, cocaine, heroine and marijuana because they are only for people who've given up on life, so if you've chosen life which I hope you have then cast your net further and explore where you can find the endocrine help and support that you need.

I have the power in me to be all that I was born to be and now I believe it !

I really get the hump when I hear 'luddite' medics rattling on about the dangers of endocrine system support and I do so because those very same 'charlatans' every day of their career abuse people in their care by default. On top of that they're only to happy to hand out in buckets or skips whichever is your choice, prescriptions for a whole host of side effect riddle concoctions. The very same concoctions that immediately place you in the:

- Psychiatric treatment trap, with all is shortfalls and associated medical/clinical abuse loops.

And

- Compromise your body's recovery processes further by their highly toxic effects upon your methylation and sulphanation processes…………arrrrrrrrrrr they make me so angry.

I am a mortal living amongst mortals and I too have rights and needs

Now it may sound astonishing but it is eminently possible that the vast majority of chronic illness perpetuation and relapse results from nothing more grandiose than toxic body syndrome *TBS*. Now I can just hear the howls of derision from the medical world, *'You joker Hardy I've never heard such tosh; toxic body syndrome, away with you man you're talking through your arse'.* Well before you the non medical readers of this book all jump the gun too, just hang on before you too commit to that assessment to You see, were I a medic I might be able to talk through my arse, but I'm not; I'm like you a former sufferer of chronic disease, therefore if you will bear with me I will explain TBS as a pragmatist and man of engineering science. TBS is a state of bodily function that prohibits optimum health because the regenerative processes and capabilities of the body are in a constant state of compromise. The very fact that a body is so compromised moves that body into a toxic bodily state, are you okay with that. You see; at the point we move into a toxic body state our expressions of disease always presents with 5 main features i.e.

1. Mood Swings.

2. Fatigue.

3. Pain.

4. Anxiety.

5. Depression.

I have the power in me to be all that I was born to be and now I believe it !

Talk, live or read about anyone with a long term chronic illness and the key presenting features of that condition will be the above and it is that phenomenon that I'm now suggesting are predictable derivatives of TBS. The reason they are predictable is because they are classic expressions of disease resulting from the deviation of normal values of hormones, neurotoxins, funguses, viruses and bacteria within any given bodily state.

You see; when any irresolvable imposition is placed upon our body, it quickly moves into a toxic state due to the break down in our methylation and sulphanation processes and as such the classic and consistent expression of that toxic state are; Mood Swings, Fatigue, Pain, Anxiety and Depression. Now talk to a medic about TBS and he or she will simply poo poo it because:

(a) They are occupationally ignorant to disease generators.

And

(b) We are still light years away from having mainstream tests and/or a medical culture etc., in place capable of looking at illness with any degree of scientific clarity.

But the reality is; at the point we as individuals begin to look at our own illness with a degree of personal clarity we begin to understand what it is we must do to aid our recovery. What I'm suggesting here is that the linear progression of chronic illness through the standard hierarchy expression of; Mood Swings, Fatigue, Pain, Anxiety and Depression is nothing more than an expression of TBS.

I am a mortal living amongst mortals and I too have rights and needs

The key to understanding TBS is to accept that it is not bacteria, micro-organisms, viral infections and fungal infections that are the greatest impediments to optimum health. It is the derivatives of those impediments in the form of neuro and bio toxins that are the greatest long term hindrance to optimum health and the intrinsically linked failure and/or underperformance of our methylation and sulphanation processes. You see it is the toxic derivatives of diseased states that;

(a) Saturate our body during disease.

And

(b) That we are unable to expel that create the TBS state.

I have the power in me to be all that I was born to be and now I believe it !

When our body however is under constant assault from neuro and bio toxins we are indeed in a state of TBS there can be no scientific argument against that. The real difficult aspect of this suggestion however; is getting to grips with the reality that in both high and low circulating TBS levels; the hierarchy expression of; Mood Swings, Fatigue, Pain, Anxiety and depression remains constant.

You see, such is the potency and potential corruptibility of TBS that our bodies are thrown out of balance very easily. Because of that it may be difficult initially or certainly prior to corrective intervention to determine whether a body is in a high or low circulating state of TBS or is simply being compromised by a high or low overall TBS load. The reason for that is that the neuro and bio toxins that underpin TBS are stored deep in body fat including the brain and it is only at the point that we begin the process of toxin removal that we begin to understand our TBS load.

TBS loading by default is unique to each individual because it's eminently possible to experience TBS from high levels of circulating toxins whilst having a relatively low overall TBS loading. The reason for that is because some of us are extremely poor at storing toxins in our body or creating additional body fat to store toxins there-in. The paradox to that is that some of us are very good at storing toxins in our body and generating additional fat to store those toxins. So that whilst there may be low circulating TBS, the originator of that circulating load can in some instances be a very high overall TBS load.

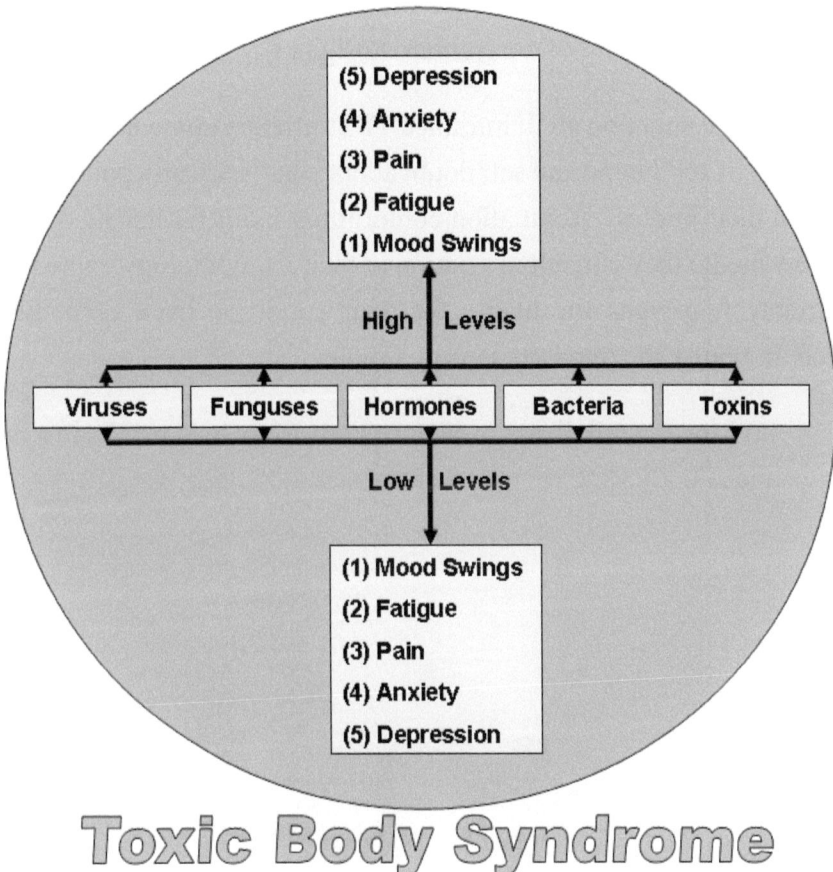

One of the main reasons that TBS is such a challenging condition is because:

>(a) Its presence is counter to all our former belief structures in terms of illness definition.

And because

I have the power in me to be all that I was born to be and now I believe it !

(b) TBS in the most part exhibits symptoms in the form of central nervous system expressions which sociologically are always regarded as being of a psychiatric origin.

In that situation all ill informed TBS sufferers immediately fall into the trap of self blame and self doubt about what's actually going wrong or on in their bodies. A situation compromised still further by the fact that any medic they consult in relation to their symtomology expression invariably re-assigns the blame for their condition back onto them. Where in reality the dynamic is very simple:

(a) Low overall diseased state and low toxin load results in a balanced body state re: fig 1 below.

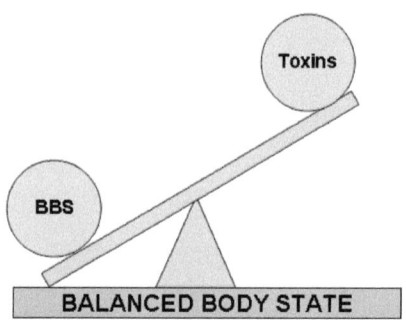

I am a mortal living amongst mortals and I too have rights and needs

Whereas

(b) A high overall diseased state and high toxin load results in a toxic body state re: fig 2 below.

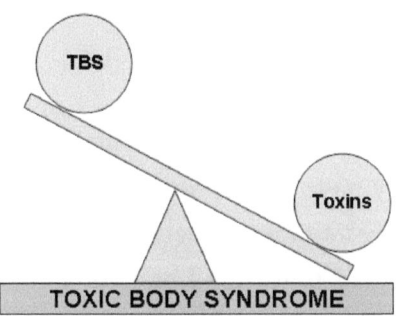

Now look I haven't just created a new acronym for the sake of it, the reason I'm bringing TBS to your attention is because actually its time that TBS was recognised. TBS is a chronic state of disease expression that is completely ignored by the medical industry and furthermore there is no effective mainstream or acceptable treatment option available to those suffering from TBS. Yet this state of bodily underperformance indiscriminately destroys lives and the quality of life and the real scary thing is that anyone of us can succumb to TBS at any point in our lives. Because whenever we move into a diseased state be that generated via a micro-organism, viral or fungal imposition and our sulphanation and methylation processes begin to falter. We potentially move into chronic TBS if our body is unable to deal or cope with the original imposition and/or its derivates e.g. toxin generation. The reason being that there is always potential for;

(a) Our cellular detox capabilities to stall completely.

(b) Our body's immune system to begin to deviate from norm.

And

(c) Our core TBS symptoms to cloud our actual clinical condition.

However be under no illusion that no matter what liver function analysis that you may have states; or how much detoxing you embark upon; TBS will be a present factor in chronic illness expression until the bodies overall TBS load is lowered or removed from the body completely. So then how do we initially test for TBS? Well you can't determine TBS via blood analysis you must undergo body fat biopsy and analysis, because that is where your TBS load resides. Okay; assuming that an excessive lipo-toxin load has been identified how do we lower it?

Well in truth and as yet I've not encountered a definitive protocol which eradicates this condition completely and believe me I've tried everything possible out there. However far infrared saunas certainly help to some degree and I'm sure that lipo-suction offers great potential, one of the areas of investigation however that I yet to personally undertake.

Nevertheless we all as individuals in our own right have to find a holistic range of techniques and protocols specifically designed to lower lipo-toxin loads which are not derivatives of ingestion detox and cleanse protocols. Because those are spectacularly unhelpful in terms of TBS eradication, simply because TBS is an insidious condition, dur to the fact it throws our entire body into a state of self destruct. When we're battling with TBS it can often feel as if everything we try to do to aid our recovery is continually disrupted by the influences of TBS.

I am a mortal living amongst mortals and I too have rights and needs

So it's not by chance that chronically ill individuals like myself move from lean muscle mass into surplus body fat generation we suffering from TBS. You see; I'm now one of those individuals who's bodily detox capabilities are so flawed that the only way my body can cope with my TBS load is to generate greater levels of body fat to encapsulate it in. The harder I work to lower my TBS load, the more toxins I release from their fat rich tomb and harder my body works to generate superfluous body fat to re-encapsulate my toxins in. The down side of that is:

(a) An increased risk of lipo diseased states.

And

(b) Every time I burn fat I'm thrown once again into intolerable TBS diseased state expression.

Nevertheless it's not all doom and gloom, my personal research and subsequent self testing in terms of lowering my own TBS expression has enabled me to enhance my own quality of life and so I'm confident that I will discover the optimum formula for lowering TBS expression in due course. For anyone diagnosed or experiencing TBS I say only this:

(a) Accept that you have a highly toxic soup trapped deep inside you.

And

(b) Do all that you can possibly do to eradicate that from you body.

But

I have the power in me to be all that I was born to be and now I believe it !

(c) Under no circumstance embark upon any radical detox or dieting campaign for there is real danger if you do of you imposing an increased health risk upon your already fragile health state.

I am a mortal living amongst mortals and I too have rights and needs

Let me be very clear here I'm in no way advocating that anyone suffering from chronic illness expression should walk away from the supervision and/or treatment protocols they're currently committed to. But what I am saying is that there is a need for a change in perceptions in and about the origin of chronic illness expression and my only hope is that at the very least my postulations enable some form of educated debate. No one should have to live with irresolvable chronic illness it is neither a karmic lesson nor an opportunity to grow. Chronic illness is nothing more than an insidious blight upon our lives and so no matter which way we or anyone from the medical/clinical industry chooses to look at it. The expression of chronic illness in society at large needs to be removed from our society and psyche completely and Amen.

If you do nothing else for the rest of the day after you've read this book I implore you to explore what I have to say from an educated and considered perspective and above all things be gentle with yourself and your body because at the end of the day, that's all we really have at our disposal. May your god and the power of your own force now take you to the place and space within your inner health where you need to go! A place that I hope now presents to you day after day; mortal beauty, hope, inspiration and love.

The road to chronic illness and TBS recovery starts with acceptance of the condition, followed only by an educated and holistic approach to lowering its insidious disease expression. Because the key to ultimate progression in anyone's pursuit of well-being is to understand that it is a toxic body that creates a toxic mind, not a toxic mind that creates a toxic body. However at the point toxins are removed from the body, the mind clears, hopes rise and fullness in life can once more be ours to enjoy free of all unnecessary pain.

I have the power in me to be all that I was born to be and now I believe it !

My Actual Healing Time Line
Time Line (a)

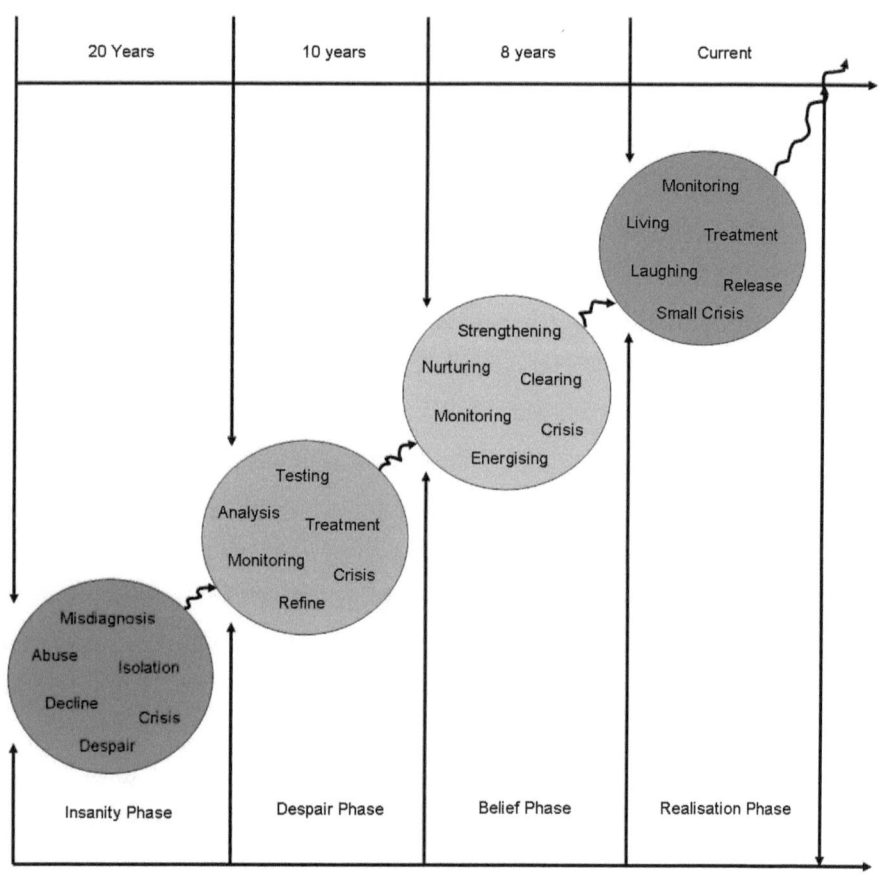

Time is only the great healer when our healing time is spent well

I am a mortal living amongst mortals and I too have rights and needs

Possible Healing Time Line
Time Line (b)

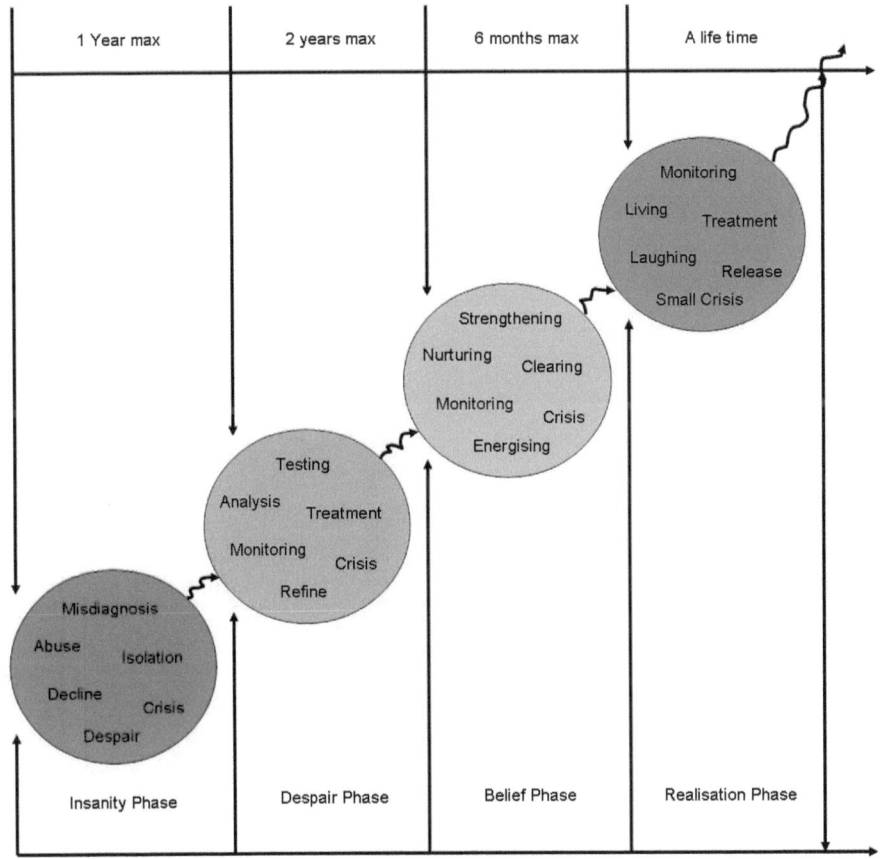

Time is only the great healer when our healing time is spent well

I have the power in me to be all that I was born to be and now I believe it !

Inappropriate Treatment Time Line 4U
Time Line (c)

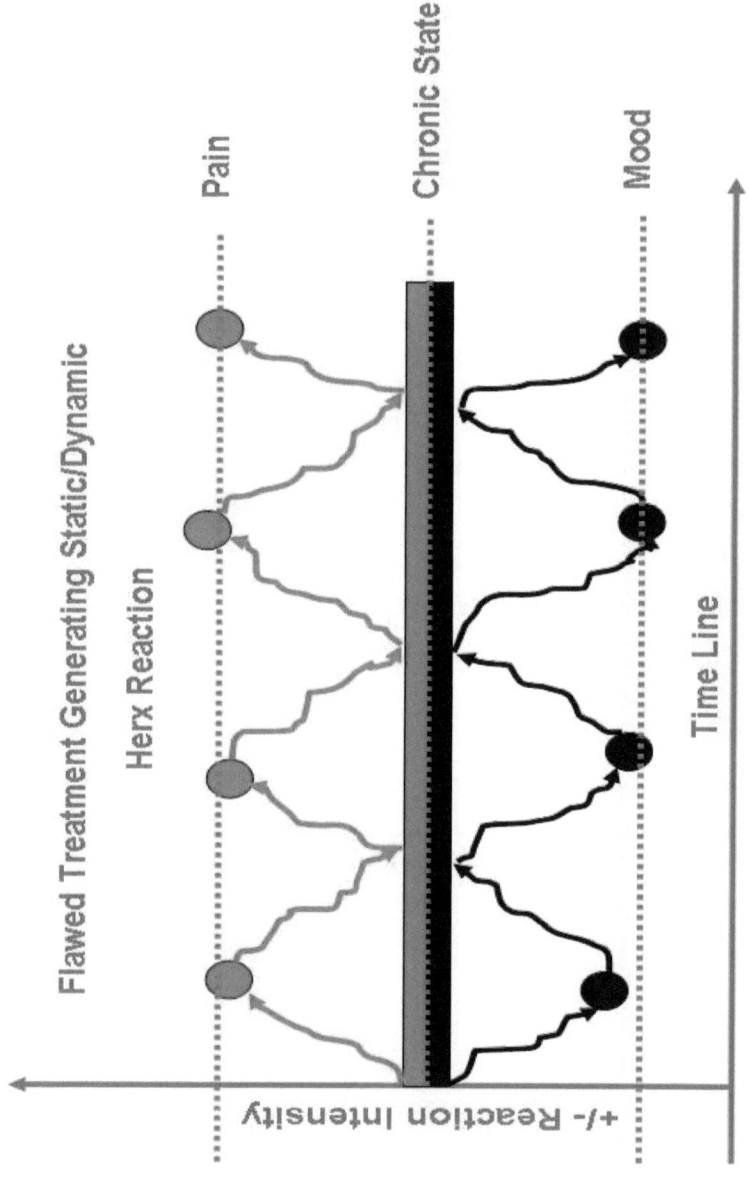

I am a mortal living amongst mortals and I too have rights and needs

Correct Treatment Time Line 4U
Time Line (d)

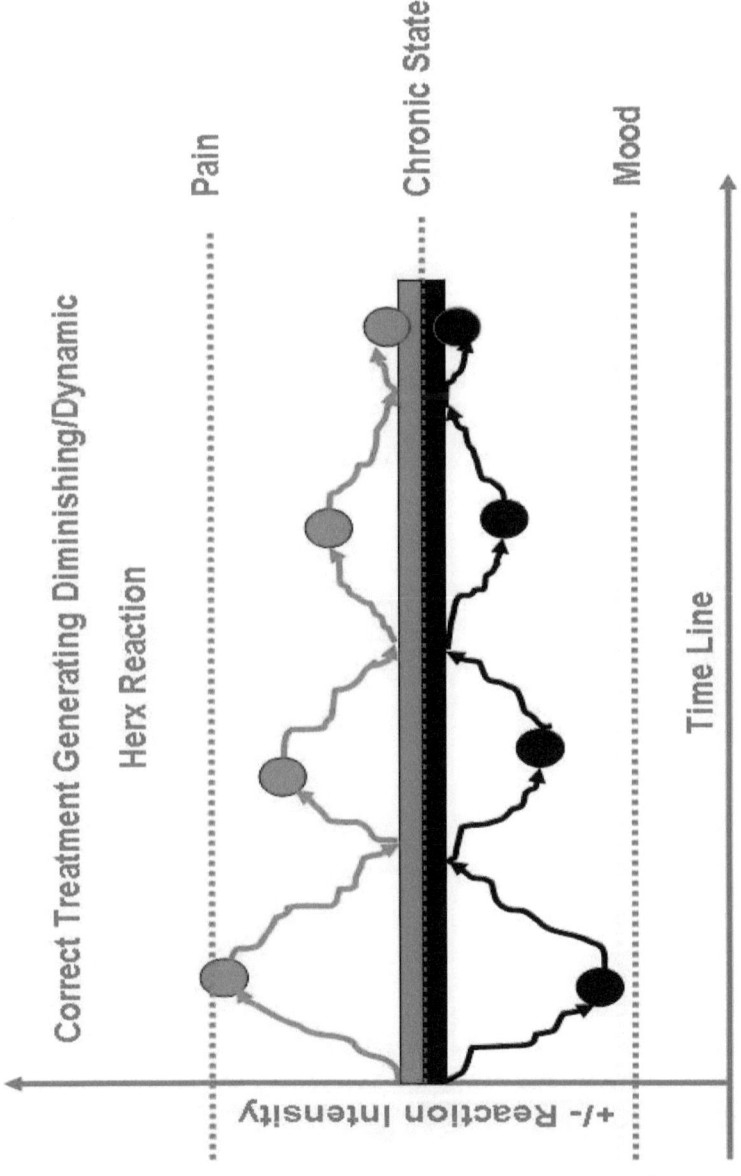

I have the power in me to be all that I was born to be and now I believe it !

I am a mortal living amongst mortals and I too have rights and needs

(11) MIND ANGER ACCEPTANCE

You know I've encountered many many very special people in my life and I'm incredibly grateful for the interactions that I've had with them all. I've been blessed to meet fine tradesmen, carers, beggars, artists, clergymen, engineers, bus drivers, road sweepers, teachers, librarians, sportsmen etc., to name just a few. Each one special and unique in their own right, each one bringing something special to my life and yet I can count on one hand the medics I've met whom I would bestow the accolade of special upon.

Yet I make no secret of the fact that whilst I will be as gracious as circumstances dictate when interacting with members of the medical industry. I nevertheless have absolutely no respect for that industry or the views of those employed within it for unless I meet a medic who is able to speak or offer a service from a point of true expertise and I don't mean legitimized bullshit. Then I'm simply not interested in what any medic has to say, and I mean, I'm not interested in anything they have to say on health, politics or any major imposition on life.

I have the power in me to be all that I was born to be and now I believe it !

You see, as far as I'm concerned they are the lowest of all mortal forms of life. The way these people conduct themselves, fail and abuse people in their care is a scandal and disgrace and for that I'm adamant that for their crimes against humanity they must pay a very heavy price, be that in this life or the next I really don't care. Until that happens I think its fine to explore in your head exactly what you would do to the rogues who've abused and failed you if you ever got the chance to deliver your own unique and personal retributions.

Now whilst some may say: *'Oh dear it's important for our souls and our recovery that we must let go of hatred and anger towards others'*. My answer is simply this, *'Explore that position again when you're tormented by a toxic liver, a toxic body and when every system and organ in your body has been damaged by an insidious bacteria, when it all could have been so easily prevented'* and then I would urge you to simply think your belief structures over again.

You see I personally believe that it's actually extremely healthy and positive to exercise your liver and brain anger. To explore just how far your emotions take you and what you think is suitable, punishment or not, for the suffering you've endured. Who knows, the very fact that you're prepared to explore those thoughts whilst accepting them for what they are, may just be an essential component of your recovery and a vital process that must not be ignored.

With that point of view in focus, I've had some lovely despicable thoughts about what I would like to do to the rogues who failed me. I so desperately want them to feel the level of pain that they create and perpetuate for people like me every minute of every day of their career. I've had thoughts of rounding all medics and their families up and transferring them to great football stadiums around the country.

I am a mortal living amongst mortals and I too have rights and needs

Where I would strap the medics into chairs and make them watch their loved ones being torn apart without mercy by Hyenas. Now obviously that would take some time because there's only so much a Hyena can eat at any given time but that's okay, the longer the suffering for all concerned the better as far as I'm now concerned. You may ask why I chose Hyenas not lions, tigers, wolfs or bears, well it's because of all the big carnivores the Hyena is in my opinion the cruelest of them all. They don't waste energy killing their victims they simply rip them apart limb from limb. I think being eaten alive and enduring unbelievable suffering before death is fine for the sort of people that I have in mind.

Now of course and after a few years naturally there wouldn't be any family or loved ones left to brutalize, so I would turn my attention directly to the medics. At which point I really would enjoy playing mind games with them torturing them day after day for years. I would inject them with all sorts of substances and break the odd one or two limbs. There would be no quarter given, no repose on grounds of mercy.

But I might allow the odd one of two to read a few books on psychology if they felt it would help them deal or cope with their physical and emotional pain. I would inject some with Lymes Disease, some with HIV, some with syphilis and some with a blend of all three. But before all of that I would revel in playing games with their head and simply talk infinitum about a whole host of things I was planning to do.

I have the power in me to be all that I was born to be and now I believe it !

The key in all my punishment regimes would be the generation of intolerable isolation, desolation and despair, creating a situation devoid of any humanistic sympathy or due diligence and care. In fact to replicate the culture that these rogues have rolled out on us for years, only in my regime there would be no 'DSBL's' written, no bullshit spoken and no postulation of care, my open and honest policy would be one of simple retribution and payback for the insidious lives that they'd lived.

Now I'm not sure if my anger towards the medical industry will ever subside but what matter that, all that I know is that I can't possibly allow my hatred of them to hold me back. I'm no longer their victim or some innocent that they can indiscriminately abuse, for I'm now 'Barry Hardy' the battle hardened medic hater who will delight in pursuing legal retribution and in due course regardless of whatever form or format that takes.

You see; I want everyone who's ever been chronically ill yet failed by the medical industry to realise and accept fully that they themselves were never to blame. In accepting that they, like me can exercise the demons that reside deep within us all after years of suffering. Because in accepting and not fighting our mind anger, I firmly believe that we're actually setting ourselves free. Simply because personal exploration as far as I'm concerned is nothing more than an intuitive expansive trait and if we choose to live in expansive state we very often leave our pain and suffering behind.

I am a mortal living amongst mortals and I too have rights and needs

Now, let me make myself clear, I would never advocate actual violence against any medical service sector worker, rogues though they are by default. Nevertheless I certainly believe and therefore think that it's healthy and positive to accept and explore our brain and liver anger because it has a vital part to play in anyone's recovery.

My only footnote would be in closing this chapter is; go gentle into that vile place and never allow yourself to be completely consumed by your cruel thoughts, just accept them for what they are.

It really is okay to hate your medical abusers and accept that they are complete 'shits, cretins and clowns'. It's okay to hate their husbands, wives and kids for reaping great rewards from being associated with and/or to those rogues.

The only point I would make is turn that hatred into positive redress and legal action and don't let it just fester or simply evaporate away. Make your formal complaints if that's what you need to do for in doing so you will kick start a myriad of much needed karmic events.

Network with fellow mindsets and empower yourself in firm assurance that you're no longer that lone foot soldier that you'd lead yourself to believe you are, because at the point you empower your psyche to engage in seeking redress, you've morphed into a dynamic and cataclysmic particle of change.

That will prove to you once and for all, that you're a very real, dramatic, even majestic vanquisher of what is an insidious blight upon society i.e. our shockingly poor and unresponsive medical model, industry and the shits who work within it who are happy to destroy far too many peoples' lives.

I have the power in me to be all that I was born to be and now I believe it !

I am a mortal living amongst mortals and I too have rights and needs

(12) SELF WORTH - NO PACTS

It doesn't matter which way we look at life in terms of the bigger scheme of things because the reality is that we're all trapped in mortality despite how immortal we may believe that we are. It is the innate fragility of mortality which is the great leveller of men, because no man ever really knows what's about to jump out on him. One moment everything is fine the next we're faced with:

- Chronic ill Health.
- Chronic Disability.
- Surgery.
- Death.

That is just the way it is and no man or woman walking this green planet is above the process or processes of mortality. Because of that we must accept at some point or at the very least come to terms with all our mortal frailties and eventualities including the fact that we will ALL die. All that we can ever hope during our own personal conclusion is that, its peaceful and that we leave our body in the knowledge that we've lived a good productive life and that we've treated and been treated with a degree of dignity and respect from our fellow man.

I have the power in me to be all that I was born to be and now I believe it !

The real difficulty for me is that in our conclusion there is always the potential for the medical world to become involved and ultimately end up playing a leading role. So where do I sit in terms of the medical industry given the theme of this book? Well exactly where my opening text in this chapter states.

I am a mortal and as a mortal I must accept all things mortal. Be that the frailty of my own body or the frailty of the men and woman charged with the responsibility for helping me with my mortality. As mortals we're never able to take just one path through mortality because events, eventualities and karmic situations completely outside of our control always impose contradictions upon us. We might strive for a given path only to find some way down the road that it's not as rewarding as we had lead ourselves to believe.

Equally the universe often conspires to place us back once more amongst energies that we'd sort to leave behind. Being trapped within mortality at times can be a very challenging existence and only those who've grown through adversity will ever truly understand that place. It's a place that has no reason, it's a place where beliefs are shattered, and it's a place where we as mortals truly understand the reality behind mortality. I believe as a mortal that there is always the potential for me to place my life in the hands of an industry that I completely despise i.e. the medical industry. But why you may ask? Well it's as simple as this; there are times in all our mortalities when we have very little choice and when reach that journeys end, all we can do is give way to our mortality and the insanity of men.

I am a mortal living amongst mortals and I too have rights and needs

In vibrancy however I neither trust nor respect the medical industry and it's as simple as that. The industry is full of contradictions, full of illusions, full of cruelty, full of incompetence and full of mortals. I will have no faith in any man or woman working within or supporting the medical industry until that industry is able to prove to me that there is an appetite within the same for change. For that industry to move away from protectionist cultures and move closer to a service delivery based upon, quality, expertise and ownership of all front end and back end service provision. My personal life passage has been too difficult, my suffering was to prolonged and the abuse I endured from those charged with the responsibility to help me was moralistically wrong.

During the production of this book I watched the Kevin Smith, 1999 film Dogma and was somewhat reminded again of the complexity and even sheer stupidity of the concept of universal divinity. In that film there are angels of all denominations happy to inflict suffering upon mortals and where God is portrayed as a complete simpleton to say the very least. It was during that film that I was vividly reminded again as if there was a need for me to connect and make personal observation in terms of the clarity between light, right, darkness and wrong. You see, given the hellish experiences thrust upon me; universal divinity is far more complex than it once was for me, because I've lived in a mortal abyss for far too many years. I can never return to the innocent that I once was, or accept that I needed to experience so much evil or mortal despair.

I have the power in me to be all that I was born to be and now I believe it !

Equally I cannot change the man I've always been and that's reflected in my daily needs, aspirations, dreams and prayers. Why I need to say my prayer every day now is completely beyond me, but I suspect deep at its root is the little boy deep within me, simply crying out to be listened to, helped and loved. Who really knows what the act of giving up prayers is all about, whether it has validity or not, all that I can say is that if it helps us at times to lower our heavy mortal loads, then perhaps at times it is worthwhile. In every man I believe there resides a god prince and dark lord, each with tremendous and equal potential, but I think the only thing that ever differentiates between those expressions is the choices that we as mortals all choose to make.

After thirty years of despair I'm of the opinion now that there is no great secret to a happy life, whether we commit to prayer or not it is a FACT that some are blessed with lots of luck whilst others are simply not. Because of that I've sort of colluded that: eagles fly with eagles, crows fly only with crows, whereas rogues on the other hand feel much happier when they can imprison the light of heart in the cesspits' they call home. That's just the way life goes I'm afraid and we just have to make the best of whatever we've been dealt, the key as ever is to retain that essential bright spark which is our personal integrity. You see, life is hard, life is cruel, life is unfair, life is love and life is always the beginning of the end. And on that final point all I'll say is; have a great day, a great life and never forget that there's nothing to fear in this life except the fear that we generate through our own silly thoughts.

I am a mortal living amongst mortals and I too have rights and needs

So please try to remember that, because life is far too short to simply lose the plot or give up and lose our way through unnecessary mind manufactured strife. Accept all that you are, all that the people who have played an important part in your life are and feel comfortable in all that you were born to be, because mortality is a collective experience and in that; NO man is free from its love or ravages. I'm happy to be who I am, I'm happy I've been able to do what I've been able to do, I'm happy to have met the people I've met along the way and that's why I know my own self worth. I will always give, care and love as much as any man can hope to do, but I'm now unwilling to engage in any process designed merely to plicate the fragile egos of those who choose to re-write my life's journey simply because that exonerates the fragilities in their own. That's why I'm happy to state:-

To those who failed me, who criticised me, who ridiculed me, to those who misdiagnosed me, who mistreated me and who clinically abused me I say to you now: may your god forgive you for all that you are for you are without doubt the lowest of all mortal life forms.

To those who could have, should have, yet chose not to heed me, to help me, to support me or to love me I say to you now, do not attempt to re-write my past by reaching out and connecting with me now or in the future. It's not for me to forgive you your prejudices, your ignorance, your selfishness or your cruelty towards me. As a mortal I merely wish for you strength, growth and humility as you pass through your own personal hells that I believe lay before you.

I have the power in me to be all that I was born to be and now I believe it !

To those who loved me, who prayed for me, who laughed with me, who cried with me and to those who died with me many times I say to you now; we may be few, but we are the luckiest of all living things. We have loved, we have cared, we have given, we have shared, we have lived and we will die touched by the presence of unquestionable friends.

To those offering up prayers for some sort of miracle or divine intervention, I say only this, never forget that you are the true master of your destiny, and whilst it's okay to sit back and rest for a while, always keep your wits, strengths and friends about you.

To those who read this book and are able to balance the many negatives with the many positives, I say only this, the truth of any mans truth is only as good as the receptivity it generates in others, so I implore you to look further for the answers you desire, because you're already on the right path for you.

To those who read this book and who find themselves fearful of everything they read, I say only this, when you release the fear that you hold deep inside, you'll discover that it's not a fear of this books contents that you have, you're simply choosing to live a life filled with fear.

To those who recognise upon completing this book that they need different help, new sources of inspiration and greater more focused support, I say only this, rejoice in all that you are because you are free of the bonds that have been holding you back, the universe and all its majesty are now yours to explore.

Above all things I believe it's important that we never ever forget that:-

- Anything and everything is possible with the right skills, the right people and the right approach.

   Therefore;

- May your health in the fullness of time return to a point where you now currently wish it to be and may you secure the level of help, love and support that we all as mortals in our own right truly deserve.

Amen

I have the power in me to be all that I was born to be and now I believe it !

Decency Warning

This warning is repeated and placed at the back of this book because if you're like my daughter you're sure to start at the back of this book and I certainly don't wish to offend any back book readers either. Therefore please don't read this book if you are easily offended by:

- Strong views.
- Strong language.
- Grammatical inconsistencies and/or poor grammar.

Or

- Personal experiences and perceptions expressed freely.

I am a mortal living amongst mortals and I too have rights and needs

Personal Notes

I have the power in me to be all that I was born to be and now I believe it !

Personal Notes

I am a mortal living amongst mortals and I too have rights and needs

Personal Notes

I have the power in me to be all that I was born to be and now I believe it !

Personal Notes

I am a mortal living amongst mortals and I too have rights and needs

Personal Notes

I have the power in me to be all that I was born to be and now I believe it !

Personal Test Results

I am a mortal living amongst mortals and I too have rights and needs

Personal Test Results

I have the power in me to be all that I was born to be and now I believe it !

Personal Test Results

I am a mortal living amongst mortals and I too have rights and needs

www.ingramcontent.com/pod-product-compliance
Ingram Content Group UK Ltd.
Pitfield, Milton Keynes, MK11 3LW, UK
UKHW041438180426
11947UKWH00007B/503